THE SMITH

The Traditions and Lore of an Ancient Craft

by

FREDERICK W. ROBINS

Fellow of the Society of Antiquaries
Fellow of the Royal Geographical Society
etc.

William Edney's wrought iron gates,
St. Mary Redcliffe, Bristol

To

ALL THE SMITHS

by name or craft,
whom I have known

F. W. R.

"From whence came Smith, albe he knight or squire,
But from the smith that forgeth at the fire?"

RICHARD ROWLANDS

Restitution of Decayed Intelligence, c. A.D. 1600

"It has always struck me that there is something highly poetical about a forge. I am not singular in that opinion: various individuals have assured me that they can never pass by one, even in the midst of a crowded town, without experiencing sensations which they can scarcely define, but which are highly pleasurable. I have a decided penchant for forges, especially rural ones, placed in some quaint quiet spot—a dingle, for example, which is a poetical place, or at a meeting of four roads, which is still more so, for how many a superstition—and superstition is the soul of poetry—is connected with these cross roads. I love to light upon such a one, especially after nightfall, as everything about a forge tells to the most advantage at night, the hammer sounds more solemnly in the stillness; the glowing particles scattered by the strokes sparkle with more effect in the darkness, whilst the sooty visage of the sastramescro, half in shadow and half illumined by the red and partial blaze of the forge, looks more mysterious and strange. . . . I believe the life of any blacksmith, especially a rural one, would offer material for a highly poetical history. . . ."

GEORGE BORROW: *Lavengro.*

ACKNOWLEDGEMENTS

The author gratefully acknowledges assistance and information given him by:

Mr. A. T. Attenborough and the Rev. G. R. Balleine (Jersey), Mr. Barnes (North Stoneham), Miss B. M. Blackwood, M.A., F.S.A. (Pitt Rivers Museum, Oxford), the late Mr. G. E. Bryant (Winchester Cathedral), Miss M. Campbell, Messrs. D. Carré (Jersey), J. Caslake (Bournemouth), H. J. S. Clark, M.A. (Wareham), J. Daniels (Boston, U.S.A.), E. C. Domoney (Iwerne Minster), the late G. Elmes, (Wareham), Gill (Taunton), F. J. and Michael Hand (Old Woking, Surrey), K. Lailey (Bradford-on-Avon), Dr. Iorwerth Peate (National Folk Museum of Wales), Messrs. T. K. Penniman, M.A., F.S.A. (Pitt Rivers Museum, Oxford), P. S. Peberdy (Tudor House Museum, Southampton), C. Robins (Jersey), Sturgeon (Poole Museum), Anthony Terry (Kemsley Newspapers), S. G. Tucker (Dorchester), Miss Dora Yates and the Gypsy Lore Society, Associated Newspapers, the smiths at Brockenhurst, Longham, St. Lawrence (Jersey) and Pontrhydfendigaid, and others he may inadvertently have omitted.

CONTENTS

Chapter I   Tubal-Cain   *Page* 13

   II   The Primitive Smith   19

   III   The Magic Metal   26

   IV   Smith Clans and Castes   32

   V   Hephaestus, the Smith-God   39

   VI   Wayland, the Hero-Smith   46

   VII   The Magic Sword   51

   VIII   Gobha, the Celtic Smith   60

   IX   The Smith-Saint   66

   X   The Mediaeval Smith   80

   XI   The Smith Guilds   89

   XII   The Post-Mediaeval Smith   99

   XIII   The Smith and the Devil   106

   XIV   Petulengro, the Gypsy-Smith   117

   XV   The Song of the Anvil   126

   XVI   Gretna Green   131

   XVII   The Smith Artist   133

   XVIII   The Smith's Fuel   139

   XIX   The Village Blacksmith   143

   Index   157

ILLUSTRATIONS

HALF-TONE PLATES

Wrought iron gates, Bristol   *Frontispiece*
Norman doorway and iron work, Barfreston   *Facing page* 32
Doorway, St. Saviour, Dartmouth   32
St. Eloi shoeing a horse   33
Memorial to a mediaeval smith   33
Works of a mediaeval clock, Salisbury   48
Vault bosses with Passion Emblems: Hammer and pincers   49
   (Winchester Cathedral)   The three nails   49
A Tudor smith: carving on a house at Ipswich   96
Shoeing a cow in the Tirol   97
Smithy, St. Lawrence, Jersey   112
"Balling iron"   113
Cow horn on bellows lever   113

LINE ILLUSTRATIONS

Ancient Egyptian forge and bellows   *Page* 23
Vulcan: plaque from Barkway, Herts   44
Saxon smithy   50
St. Dunstan and the Devil   68
St. Eloi   70
Twelfth century smithwork   81
Arms of the Worshipful Company of Farriers   91
Clock works from Bere Regis church   104
An eighteenth century blacksmith's sign   138
Bicycle, made in 1872   146
The blacksmith-cricketer. Cartoon by "Neb"   148
The fringed apron   150

TUBAL-CAIN

The hands and nails and teeth—these were man's weapons of old,
After these, stones and the branches of trees that grow in the forest,
And, too, of flaming fire he sought—when its uses were known.
LUCRETIUS: *On the Nature of Things.*

IF THE discovery of the means of producing fire was, as the
author has maintained elsewhere, the most momentous discovery man has ever made—more momentous certainly than
any modern scientific discovery so far—the discovery of the
means of smelting metallic ores and of working them is not far
behind in importance. It is closely associated with and was
certainly dependent on the production of fire, but, whereas
the latter was obviously suggested by the observation of
natural phenomena, the actual inception of metallurgy is
shrouded to a large extent in mystery.

It is generally agreed that the smelting even of copper and
bronze could not have taken place at an ordinary open fire,
yet, if it did not, how came it into men's minds to build a
special furnace for the smelting of ore which could not in itself
have indicated what the product would be? Some accidental
raising of the fire temperature above normal and an accidental
melting down of the copper-bearing ore seems to be suggested.
True, a certain amount of native metal was available at first,
but not sufficient to be of much practical use, and the native
metal would not have led to the deliberate smelting of ore for
metal production, any more than the natural fires of volcanoes
and lightning would have taught man how to produce fire for
himself.

Somehow or other, though, the idea of a forced draught
was hit upon, the initial application, apparently, being in the
building of special hearths on a windy hillside in such a way
as to induce a natural draught to activate the flame and raise
the heat. Examples of these, dating from as late as Roman
times, have been found in Cumberland and elsewhere, but Dr.
W. A. Timperley has recently found pits containing charcoal,

ash, slag and ironmelt, on valley sites, at Norton, Sheffield, earlier in date than some of the hillside smelting pits. An Early Bronze Age smith's furnace found at Agnaskeagh, Ireland, and dating from about 1800 B.C., had a horizontal flue for the draught.

As early as the Fifth Dynasty in Egypt—some six thousand years ago—however, forced draught was applied, by means of blowpipes, to broken ore mixed with charcoal in a heap on the ground or in a shallow pit.[1] Ernest Mackay, in *The Indus Civilisation*, refers to copper ores being found, but no furnaces in which they could have been reduced, suggesting, therefore, the heating of the ore, with charcoal, in a hole, by means of a blast. It was not until the Eighteenth Dynasty in Egypt, some three thousand three hundred years ago, that the bellows appeared, but that was in good time for the advent of ironworking, which requires a higher temperature, but which is only three thousand years old in the parts where it occurs at the earliest known date—that is, of course, apart from the working of lumps of meteoric iron into small objects, mostly for ornament.

While, at the outset, copper objects were wrought by hammering the crude copper cold, it was not long before the better method of casting was adopted, the moulds being of clay or stone, anything requiring to have a sharp edge being no doubt hammered afterwards.

There is a distinct copper period in Egypt and Western Asia, but in most other parts of the world the Neolithic (late Stone) Age is succeeded immediately by an epoch in which there is a growing use of bronze, an amalgam of copper and tin, usually in the approximate proportion of nine parts to one. World epochs are not usually clear-cut, and the use of stone implements, stone arrowheads in particular, went on after the introduction of bronze, for some time. In the same way, there was a marked use of bronze for many purposes well into the age of Iron.

Copper deposits are fairly widespread and not infrequently tin is found in juxtaposition with it, so that the alloy could fairly easily be stumbled upon, either by the accidental smelting of some tin ore with the copper ore,[2] or, as Mr. Lucas

[1] *Ancient Egyptian Materials and Industries* (Lucas).
[2] A Phrygian tradition, quoted by Schliemann, ascribed the discovery of the fusing of metals to accidental melting in a forest fire!

would have it, by the deliberate addition of tin ore to the copper. The incidence of the deposits, even if the knowledge was diffused from a common source, lends itself to the carrying on of the industry in many localities by native metal workers. With iron, it seems to have been different, and, while many archaeologists aver that bronze working came into our own parts through the invasion of a race or races possessing the necessary knowledge, there is not the same evidence of its practitioners being aliens to the races among whom they worked as there is in many cases with the blacksmiths.

On the other hand, one cannot overlook the fact that a smith in archaic society was usually a worker in all kinds of metals, for all kinds of purposes, and not a specialist, so that, with the advent of ironworking, either the bronze smith adapted himself to the new material, and to new methods—since iron was wrought and not cast until a very late stage in history—or else he went out of business, and the iron smith took on the bronze working as well. So, too, the ironworker was often a worker in the precious metals as well, notwithstanding the fact that gold, being found in its pure state, antedated in use the more utilitarian metals. In some cases, however, there is evidence that, almost from the beginning, the goldsmith was a separate and superior worker to the bronze and iron smith, notably in ancient Egypt, where a goldsmith appears to have been held in high repute, contrasting with the very lowly position held by the ordinary artisan. The uses to which the precious metal was put made its working a definite art—yet it was not long in the world's history before the metal workers in general, and the copper and bronze workers in particular, became artists as well as craftsmen.

Mr. V. G. Childe, in *Scotland Before the Scots*, maintains that bronze smelting in the Early Bronze Age was generally done only on the ore fields, since there only are the slag heaps found, and that the product, in Europe, at this stage, was purveyed by itinerant smiths, who travelled with half-finished articles to be finished off to the taste of the producer. To Scotland these merchant artificers came from Ireland, presumably carrying their tools, including stone anvils and hammer stones, with them. In the Bronze Age village of Jarlshof, in the

Shetland Isles, there are three stages of industrial culture: (1) no
bronze, (2) a bronze smith set up his workshop in the village,
making swords, axes and knives in clay moulds, and (3) there
is slag evidence of ironworking, though bronze implements were
being cast at the same time. The smith who started his business
there in the Late Bronze Age turned an ordinary dwelling into
a smithy. Mr. Childe thinks he must have come from Ireland,
or had been trained in an Irish school, as his forms are Irish.
Having started his smithy at Jarlshof, he became a resident
smith, trading no doubt not only with the village but with the
surrounding islands. His tools, judging from general finds in
Britain, included hammers, anvils, cold chisels, pointed awls
and stone moulds.

In the archaic world, smiths had been mostly itinerant and
welcome visitors, even in Homeric Greece, very much as the
gypsy smith is in the east of Europe, but from the later Bronze
Age onwards they tended to settle, perhaps, as Mr. Childe
suggests, forced to do so by the gradually increasing competition of iron, or, more probably, one thinks, because of the
greater call for their services with the increased use of metal,
especially if they became workers in both the main materials.
Tubal-Cain was far from being alone in working bronze and iron
too, if indeed the mention of iron is not a later interpolation
in the Old Testament reference, and the Jarlshof smith was
still casting bronze swords and axes after iron smelting started
there. One has the analogy of the rural iron founder of the
present century, and the blacksmith, turning their foundries
and workships into garages and motor repair depots, to meet
the changing times. As Gertrude Bell wrote,[1] "Necessity shall
speak with an authority unknown to that borrowed wisdom
which men obey or discard at will."

Apart from the fact that alternative metals were available,
the more profuse supply and distribution of iron ores rendered
iron implements more readily available and cheaper than those
in bronze; indeed in China bronze was rarely used by any but
the wealthier folk, and by them mainly for weapons. It would
seem, too, that iron was primarily used in Europe for the
production of weapons. "Cheap iron," says Gordon Childe,
"released new forces of destruction and made formidable

[1] *The Desert and the Sown.*

weapons as generally available as efficient tools."[1] Hence, probably, the power of the smith and of the races who knew iron. Truly the more modern a thing is the more ancient it is![2] Science in the twentieth century is all too frequently accused of prostituting its knowledge by directing it into destruction instead of construction. So, too, in the prehistoric ages, the coming of metal, which should have meant and did mean so much in improving life, making it easier and preserving it, looms much more prominently in the records, at any rate as a means of destruction, not only of the life of an animal which may provide sustenance for that ostensibly superior being, Man, but also of the lives of enemies, real or potential rivals, intruders, even perhaps perfectly innocent strangers and unwanted fellow humans generally!

Spears, arrowheads, axes, daggers, swords—these, whether for hunting or otherwise, are the common finds in the remains of the early metal ages. Yet the advent of metals meant many other things besides—the digging stick or the forked stick which was the ancestor of the plough is tipped with metal at first, and then becomes a metal implement with wooden accessories. Boats are shaped with tools instead of being laboriously burnt out. Forests are cleared to make room for cultivation; without the metal axe the felling of a single tree was a difficult task. Workship, field and kitchen alike are equipped with tools which are not only more varied but more efficient, speedier and more precise in action than the old implements of stone, wood and bone.[3] Not least of all, the earthen pot, into which heated stones were cast to bring the water to boil, is developed into the metal cauldron, to become through many ages the all-purpose cooking-pot of the peasant, the one possession without which a peasant household in China, and elsewhere, was completely "lost", an article so valuable among Greek and Celt alike as to figure as a symbol of housekeeping and a standard of wealth, and so indispensable as to rattle at the saddle bow of the Eastern nomad. All these were products of the smith.

[1] Including armoured vehicles! . . . "and the Lord was with Judah and he drave out the inhabitants of the mountain; but could not drive out the inhabitants of the valley because they had chariots of iron" (Judges i, 19).
[2] Recent discoveries have shown Sheffield to have been an ironworking centre centuries before the Roman occupation.
[3] Og, King of Bashan, even had a bedstead of iron (Deut. iii, 11).

Despite the wide occurrence of iron ores, there have been races who have had to import their iron; more still have found it more convenient to do so. Twelfth-century Formosans were able to build forges but not to smelt crude iron ore, so they raided the Chinese mainland for iron and valued it so highly that spears tipped with it had a line attached with which to draw them back after being thrown. Ironworking, indeed, seems, in most cases, to have been "diffused knowledge"; an African folklore story tells of man copying it from a god, and the evidences of introduction by, and even monopoly by, alien races are profuse. Even Tyre imported iron from Tarsus in Cilicia (Ezekiel xxvii, 12). "Diffusion", indeed, often meant, in this case, not the imparting of knowledge, but the infiltration of alien smiths, who kept their craft a close mystery.

Whatever may be the ultimate fate of Chinese culture and belief, there is much in it of eternal wisdom.

"It is laughable," wrote H. A. Franck,[1] in 1923, "to think of us children among nations worrying about . . . one thousands of years old which . . . may still be ambling her own way long after we have disappeared from the face of the earth. Some of us are frankly tired of politics."

Some of us certainly are. The dual functions of the ironworker are epitomized in Chinese mythology, which has two personages spoken of and depicted as men with a bull's head and obviously related—Shên-nung, the Divine Harvestman, who introduced agriculture, and Ch'e-you, the inventor of arms, and the Master of War. It is the latter, though, who, according to Granet, represents the forge deified. Nevertheless, the functions of the smith throughout the world and its ages have been, and are, mainly twofold—agricultural and martial—with the addition of later sidelines such as domestic furnishing and transport. Picture, though, a world without metal working! Less warlike? Perhaps not, though wars might not be so deadly. Life would certainly be harder, more precarious. Such is the value of the original smith—Tubal-Cain, the "instructor of every artificer in brass and iron"[2]—and his kind.

---

[1] *Wanderings in North China.*
[2] Genesis iv, 22. Tradition gives the Kenites as descendants of Tubal-Cain, and Jael, who slew Sisera with a nail, as the wife of a smith.

CHAPTER II

THE PRIMITIVE SMITH

How strangely gleams through the gigantic trees
The red light of the forge. Wild beckoning shadows
Stalk through the forest ever and anon,
Rising and bending with the flickering flame
Then flitting into darkness.

LONGFELLOW: *The Spanish Student.*

AMONG primitive folk, both of ancient and modern times, the smith was, and is, often his own iron smelter. In the north of Europe, the source of the prehistoric production of iron was always bog ore, and this has been used in Norway and Sweden continuously, up to recent times; iron smelting there was a recognized farm industry, carried on at certain times of the year, in primitive forms. The ore was burned in a funnel-shaped hollow dug in the ground and lined with clay, bellows being fixed on opposite sides of the pit, inclined so as to blow down into it. The fuel was good dry wood, perhaps mixed with a little charcoal. The iron so produced was poor, and the slag had to be hammered out in the smithy.[1]

Though ironworking in most of Negro Africa is not of a great age and most native traditions imply its introduction from elsewhere, the methods employed throw an interesting light on primitive technique. In the case of the Elgeyo of East Africa, the prehistoric picture is almost complete: not only was their smelting done by their smiths, but the latter were itinerant. Their furnace was an oven resembling an anthill in shape, built of mud over a hole, the furnace itself being in the hole, and fanned by bellows. Having produced the iron, the smiths forged it into iron weapons. Originally the trade was hereditary, sons invariably following their fathers as smiths, but in the twentieth century they are not doing so, and the trade is dying out under the impact of imported materials.[2]

The metal worker's profession is also dying in other

[1] *Scandinavian Archaeology* (Shetelig and Falk).
[2] *Cliff Dwellers of Kenya* (J. A. Massam, 1927).

19

quarters in Africa for similar reasons, and smiths become difficult to find. In former days, among the Lambas of Northern Rhodesia, the metal had to be won from the earth by primitive methods, and the men who held the secret could command wealth and influence. To learn the "mystery" of ironworking, the embryo smith had to serve an apprenticeship, living with his teacher, watching his working and helping by making the fire and manipulating the bellows. The apprentice helped to build the smelting-house, and only after he had gone through a period of menial work did he begin to forge, first axes, then spears, and then hoes. Apprenticeship and probation over, he could then set up his own establishment. The payment made to the master-smith was small, perhaps some beads only, as while the apprentice was learning he was providing free assistance; also he supplied his own raw materials and the finished articles at first belonged to the master, who could sell them for his own reward.[1]

In Dahomey, smithing is co-operative; a group of iron-workers attached to a forge work in turn on the implements required by each member. The forged product belongs to the one whose iron was being forged, and he sells it for his own benefit, while taking his turn in working on the products of the others.

As, no doubt, would have been the case in prehistoric times, there were inhibitions to be observed in connection with such an important operation as smelting. The Lamba smith might have no intercourse with his wife on the night before, or the metal would remain soft and not harden, though helpers did not come under the prohibition. Women might not enter the smelting-place, but were permitted to bring food to the smelters and place it outside the chamber.[2] Similar prohibitions obtain elsewhere; the Ankola smith might not have intercourse with his wife, nor come near a menstruating woman, during smelting operations.

The Lamba smith, with his helpers, dug for ore, finding detached nodules, which they broke up; as soon as a quantity was gathered, some of the helpers collected dry boughs of a certain tree which, when burnt, forms charcoal, while others

[1] *The Lambas of Northern Rhodesia* (C. M. Doke).
[2] Ibid.

commenced to build a tent-like smelting-house, with poles for the frame, and grass thatching tied over the poles. When the roof was finished, a hole about three feet deep was dug in the floor, and a mud wall about a foot high built around it, with six openings for the insertion of the bellows' nozzles. Charcoal was then put at the bottom of the hole, followed by a layer of ore,[1] and alternate layers of charcoal and ore until the hole was filled. Fire having been set to the charcoal, six men worked the bellows, the latter made of sewn-up buckskins, with, at one end, a hollow piece of wood, secured by a bond of bark rope, the nose of the wood tube being inserted into a nozzle-shaped piece of antheap passed through the opening in the wall; at one time the tube was of burnt clay.

The bellows was gripped at the base by one foot of the assistant, while at the opening at the top were fixed two pieces of wood, with slots, made with leather and thongs, for the insertion of two fingers in front and the thumb behind, the bellows, by this means, being worked up and down. As the mass in the pit subsided, so it was replenished with charcoal and ore. The operation was carried on until late in the day, and, at the finish, the master knocked away the clay wall to inspect the metal. Prodding it out with green poles, he put it in a safe place for the night. In the morning he knocked the metal lump with an iron ball in shrunken skin, to break off the dross and slag, storing pieces of the clean metal for use. He might have as many as ten men helping him collect ore and charcoal, paying, for their services, each unmarried man an axe-head and each married man an axe-head and hoe—an unusual example of higher wages for married men! The bellows workers were unpaid volunteers, who worked in relays for the sheer enjoyment of the thing.

The iron having been produced, the smith chose a place for his forge where there was a big strong stone on which he could hammer the metal, putting over it a shelter of branches and making a fire of charcoal on the ground. If his assistants were not learners, their services were paid for; usually there would be two of them. In the first part of the operation, one assistant worked the bellows, and the other, when the smith had put the

[1] A similar method is believed to have been employed in prehistoric copper smelting.

red-hot metal on the stone, with a piece of green bark for tongs, hammered it, under the master's direction. As it cooled it was put back on the fire and worked again until the required shape was attained; the master-smith's job was to straighten and finish off the implement, with the aid of two hammers, one being entirely of metal, the other with a metal head and wood handle.

Small smithies were often erected in the village for sharpening, mending and straightening implements, but the actual manufacture from the crude metal never took place in these.[1] The Hausa method of smelting iron is very similar to that of the Lambas, except that the smelting takes place in a burnt clay cylinder, about two feet in diameter, two inches thick and four feet high, with a hole at the bottom, instead of a mere hole in the ground.[2] A few African tribes have no bellows, but merely ventilating tubes at ground level, withdrawn as the fire gains force. In other cases the fire is started by the bellows, but afterwards the ventilating tubes are relied upon. Furnaces are usually conical or cylindrical, in some cases actual termite nests. Bellows vary in form and manipulation from race to race.

There are cases where races having their own smiths do not smelt their own metal, either because they cannot or because they find it more convenient to buy it. The former was the case in old Formosa, whose smiths got their iron from the Chinese mainland; the Wachagga of East Africa got their iron from a neighbouring tribe.[3]

The primitive forge was frequently a mere hole in the ground, plainly showing its descent from the domestic hearth. Sometimes it was backed by a large stone, as in the case of the Nagas of the Assam-Burma frontier, and the Chuka smithy in Kenya—the latter with two smaller stones to keep in position the pottery nozzle of the bellows.[4] A little more advanced is the Hunza forge—a few stones built up to contain the charcoal fire, with a neat hollow tube of soapstone beside it, into which the bellows play.[5]

The common anvil is a large hard stone, as in the case of the

[1] *The Lambas of Northern Rhodesia* (C. M. Doke).
[2] *Antiquity*, Vol. XV, p. 289.
[3] *Kilimanjaro and its People* (Dundas).
[4] *Vanishing Tribes of Kenya* (Maj. G. St. J. O. Browne).
[5] *Language Hunting in the Karakoram* (E. O. Lorimer).

Lambas, and often the smith sits at his work, as he may be seen doing in Greek vase paintings. Hammer, tongs, chisel and file are the practically universal basic tools of his craft.

In the India of the Vedas, the blacksmith's fire was *fanned.* "The smith with well-dried wood, with anvil, and with feather fan to activate the flame."[1] This was the case, too, with early hearths of ancient Egypt, though there is a tomb painting, dating from Thothmes III, showing a smelting furnace being blown by means of bellows very similar to some used in Negro Africa; the two blowers have each one foot on a round bellows, obviously working the pair alternately, with cords in their

Ancient Egyptian forge and bellows

hands with which to pull the air vessel out after compression. The pair of air tubes on either side are connected into a single nozzle.[2]

Primitive smiths of historic ages and the present day, no matter how archaic their methods may be, almost universally employ the bellows, usually of goatskin, sometimes the skin of some other animal. In classical times and lands, goatskins were used, and tanned ox-skins for larger bellows, which were worked by means of a lever. The Chuka bellows consist of two triangular-shaped flat skin bags, with pottery nozzles, and two sticks sewn along the edges, with loops to take the fingers of the blower: the bellows are worked alternately, one hand for each,

[1] *Vedic India* (Ragozin, 1895).
[2] *Vide* Neuburger, *The Technical Arts of the Ancients.*

the hands being raised and depressed in turn, and each bag being opened and closed about twenty times a minute.[1]

The Hunza bellows, too, are double, two goatskin bags each fitted with a nozzle at one end, at the other end being two wooden lips that open as one raises the hand and meet tightly in the fist as one presses down, these, too, being worked alternately.[2] Further east in Asia, however, other materials are used. The Naga bellows consist of a pair of vertical tubes of bamboo, with a pump fitting into them composed of a cane covered with bits of old cloth or chicken feathers held in place by more cane.[3] The bellows of the Lakhers (Thibet) are rather similar: two hollowed-out logs about four feet long each has a hole pierced at the bottom holding a hollow bamboo to carry the blast produced by a piston of stick-work in the log and made airtight by being bound with cloth or feathers.[4] In most cases the blowing is done by an assistant or assistants, but in the case of the smiths working for the Hunzas the peasant for whom the work is being done has to do the blowing.

Charcoal is, *par excellence*, the fuel of the blacksmith. If a Lakher wants the smith to make him a dao or a hoe, he buys the iron, and takes enough charcoal for the fire, and such a provision does not seem to be uncommon. Among the Wachagga of East Africa, smithing is confined to certain clans; in the Malissa clan, the eldest son becomes a smith, the next a charcoal burner, the third a smith, and so on alternately, but if the second son had sons, the eldest must become a smith again, but he must pay a fee of a heifer and a goat, as paid by all who wish to become smiths and are not of the smiths' clan. One clan are all charcoal burners through not having paid the fee. Despite this provision for "professional" charcoal burning, however, the charcoal is mostly made by the person requiring an article forged, and supplied to the smith, as well as the metal for two such items, the duplicate being for the smith himself, or the second may be replaced by a goat. In the case of weapons, three have to be made.[5]

This method of payment is reminiscent of milling practice

[1] *Vanishing Tribes of Kenya* (Major Browne).
[2] *Language Hunting in the Karakoram* (E. O. Lorimer).
[3] *The Sema Nagas* (Hutton). *The Angami Nagas* (Hutton).
[4] *The Lakhers* (Parry).
[5] *Kilimanjaro and its People* (Dundas).

in mediaeval England, but other methods are more common. Often payment is made in grain or stock, but at one time Elgeyo (East Africa) smiths were not allowed to hold stock, as the other tribesmen feared that if they became wealthy they might give up the work, so payments were made to them in food.[1]

The Indian village blacksmiths receive a share of the harvest for their services. Some of the Lakhers buy their metal work from outsiders, but where there are village blacksmiths these receive certain dues from the villagers in consideration for keeping their tools in order and making new tools—daos, knives, hoes and axes.[2] Among the Hunzas, too, each Burusho household pays a small yearly tax to the Bericho community of smiths, and in return the blacksmiths tour the villages once or twice a year and make or mend whatever may be required.[3]

The main products of the African or Asiatic blacksmiths are significant—agricultural implements, especially hoes, and weapons, with the former the more regular industry among settled peoples. In India, as elsewhere, the connection between the smith and agriculture is close, and at the seed-sowing ceremony of the Nilagiris, on the day of full moon, the black-gold- and silversmiths construct separate forges in the temple, each making something according to his craft.[4]

[1] *Cliff Dwellers of Kenya* (J. A. Massam, 1927).
[2] *The Lakhers* (Parry).
[3] *Language Hunting in the Karakoram* (E. O. Lorimer).
[4] *Omens and Superstitions of Southern India* (Thurston, 1912).

CHAPTER III

THE MAGIC METAL

And of the marvellous power of four-leaved clover and horseshoes,
With whatsoever also was writ in the lore of the village.
LONGFELLOW: *Evangeline.*

MANY people today treasure a horseshoe or a representation of
one as a bringer of good luck, or will pick up a pin for the same
reason, without realizing that they are perpetuating a very
ancient belief in the magic properties of iron, dating from even
before the general advent of ironworking.

Meteoric iron was known and used long before iron smelting
commenced. Naturally enough, a material which dropped from
the skies could only be a gift of the gods. Meteoric iron, known
to the ancient Egyptians as "bia", was regarded by them as
supernatural and connected with the Storm-god, Seth; just as
the Storm-god Balicho in South-West Asia was, too, connected
with iron. In Egypt, while the scarcity of meteoric iron did not
permit of its use for ordinary tools, its divine origin was
sufficient reason for its use for the instruments used by the
priests for the "Opening the Mouth" ceremony performed on
the mummy[1] during the funeral ceremony and before its place-
ment in the tomb—a ceremony designed to enable the soul to
give the correct answers to the doorkeepers of the underworld.

Apart from such a direct suggestion as the dropping of the
metal from the skies, the closely guarded secrets of metallurgy
in themselves created an aura of mystery and superstition
around it, which began before the advent of iron. Referring to
certain legendary races of Asia Minor renowned for their metal
working, Schliemann, in his *Ilios*, wrote:

"They are nothing else than the representatives of an
identical metallic industry symbolised in its progressive
developments; that the religion of Samothrace was, in the
beginning, nothing but a simple institution of mysteries

[1] *Antiquity*, Vol. X, 23.

26

founded on metallurgy and presided over by Thea, whose priests were, in fact, metallurgists. These ministers, having transmitted the blessing of the goddess to other men, were deified from gratitude."

More probably, of course, from awe, which is rather less ephemeral than gratitude!

Be that as it may, the patent fact remains that, from the outset, metal working was regarded, like its parent, firemaking, as a gift of the gods—or of demons. Barotseland folklore tells how Kamunu, the first man, copied ironworking from Nyambi, the god[1]; in Northern Rhodesia, the Bakaande Bantus say that the Creator instructed their early ancestors in metal working, while the Basuto claim that their first ancestor was Noto (hammer), son of Morizong (smith). The Klein Letaba believe that they were created holding in their hands the instruments of the smith.[2]

In the Lepcha (Himalayan) story of the bringing of fire to the world, it was to the demon blacksmiths that the messengers had to go to procure it. In the Burmese story of the two Nats or spirits who were brother and sister, the latter renowned for her beauty, the brother was a blacksmith, the strongest man in the country, the blow of whose hammer on the anvil made the earth tremble, and whose forge was the mouth of Hell.

In India, the Gond clans of the Deccan worship an iron spearhead, as a symbol of the clan god, and their mythology contains stories of how their sacred pieces of iron were acquired. Both they and the Koyas attach ritual importance to iron weapons and implements, which Dr. C. von Furer-Harmendorf regarded as evidence of their having been the introducers of iron to primitive tribes of the Deccan in a pre-metal (or preiron?) age.[3] In parts of Africa, there are rites connected with the bringing into use of a new anvil or hammer, and the Japanese blacksmith worships the god of his bellows and gives them a day of rest every year, though this may be more from the animistic outlook which causes him to ascribe a spirit or soul to every object of daily use than from any particular veneration of his craft.

---

[1] *Barotseland* (Smirke).
[2] *Mining and Metallurgy in Negro Africa* (Walter Cline).
[3] *Man*, August, 1948.

The belief in the power of iron to ward off evil is widespread, in fact almost universal. Demons in India, afrits in Arabic countries, witches and warlocks, hobgoblins, spirits and the like further west[1]—all are afraid of its power and can be kept away by it. When a storm seems imminent in the Abruzzi, the peasant women hastily snatch up all the iron implements, carefully removing the wooden handles, and throw them on the threshing floor, contriving to drop some of them in the shape of a cross, and recite a prayer. As a last resource, they may take out the iron chain which holds up the cauldron over the fire and shake it vigorously.[2] The Devil, seeing it, is alarmed, remembering when he was chained up in Hell—but the real reason lies beyond that, in the old pagan belief in the magic power of iron.

Iron and steel are safeguards against the power of supernatural beings in the Highlands of Scotland; when you enter a fairy dwelling, you should stick a piece of steel, a knife, a needle, or the like, in the door, for then the elves cannot shut the door until you come out again. A knife or a nail will keep the fairies from lifting you or your children. Even in this twentieth century, an old Dorset villager had a scythe blade and a sickle over his bed, to keep off witches. Not so long ago, too, schoolboys would seal a bargain by touching "cold iron"!

In Morocco, a knife or a dagger may be placed under a sick man's pillow, because the steel keeps away demons. The Sinhalese, if carrying food from one place to another, put a nail on it, lest a demon should affect the viands; and if a man has a sore on his body he puts a piece of iron on it as a protection against demons. Iron ornaments on a child's ankles, or iron chains around his neck, in Africa, are there to prevent devils from entering the little body,[3] though, contradictorily, the magical force inherent in iron is regarded as inimical to life and peace.

Strangest of all these beliefs, perhaps, is the one enshrined in Lapp tales of youths who encounter troll maidens of outstanding beauty and turn them into mortal wives by throwing steel—usually a knife—over the desired. On this same principle, if a Lapp sees one of the supernatural herds of reindeer, he

---

[1] The ghost of a murdered man was said to have sat on a gate at Shillingstone, Dorset, until it was replaced by an iron one!

[2] *Home Life in Italy* (Lina Duff Gordon).

[3] *The Golden Bough* (Frazer).

nust throw steel—again, usually a knife—or brass rings over
limself, and the animals will then become real reindeer which
1e may keep. Bear hunters, too, are arrayed in brass rings and
:hains by their womenfolk.[1]

Naturally, his mastery of the magic material and its craft
nvests the smith himself with magical powers, increased,
iccording to Christina Hole,[2] by his association with fire and
1is position as a servant of the sacred horse. More particularly
:he former, the author would suggest, as the reverence extends
:ar beyond the cult of the sacred horse and fire is universally
;acred. Sometimes smiths were the repositories of secret charms
to heal wounds. Did they, perchance, practise cauterization?
Thurston, in his *Omens and Superstitions of Southern India*,
relates that a blacksmith knocked out the teeth of a wizard to
take his power from him—which brings the smith into dentistry
as well!

Tissot, in *Unknown Switzerland* (1889), tells a story of a
chamois hunter with a reputation of friendship with the devil;
the hunter was also apparently something of a smith. An
Englishman asked to be shown the devil, so after some demur
the hunter took him to a cellar where he had a little forge, which
he lit. He made an enormous fire and went several times
around, reciting magic formulae. At last, approaching the
expectant Englishman, he presented his purse. "The Devil,
well if you wish to see him, my lord, he is in there"—and the
story ends with the Englishman paying—in metal, of course—
to dispel the Devil.

That story may be apocryphal, but it is in line with powers
attributed to the forge in many parts. Even St. Patrick prayed
to be protected from the incantations of "women, smiths or
druids": it is not recorded which he regarded as the worst, but
the order may be significant! The smith-gods of the ancient
Irish were regarded as gifted with magic, and in some parts, to
this day, the smith is regarded by the peasantry as possessed
of something of the powers of his predecessors in the craft,
sorcerers and necromancers[3]—all of which seems a curious

[1] *Lapland* (H. A. Bernatzik).
[2] *English Folklore.*
[3] *Celtic Myth, Legend, Poetry and Romance* (Chas. Squire), and *Ulster
Journal of Archaeology*, Vol. IX, 1861–2.

contradiction to the concurrent belief in the enmity between iron and things supernatural. The Irish, however, always seem illogical to the Englishman, and they were not alone in this apparent contradiction.

Gypsies are sorcerers and fortune-tellers, as well as smiths, and the Dactyli, the fabled Phrygian sons of Rhea, celebrated as metallurgists, were also enchanters and practised spells and mysteries. The repellent virtues of iron, indeed, seem to have been more effective against immortals than mortals.

In Africa it is usual for a smith to have attributed to him some supernatural power. The Chagga smiths of East Africa are feared on account of a curse they are able to invoke by their bells; a smith's bell must not be touched by anybody but himself or his eldest son.[1] Chuka smiths are believed specially gifted in magic, and old pottery nozzles from their bellows are potent charms.[2] On the other side of the dark continent, the Nri guild of blacksmiths in Nigeria, craftsmen and priests, as the smiths of Samothrace were said to have been, owned an oracle.

What people do not understand, they revere, fear, or both. So it was with the mysterious material of power, iron. Side by side with the recourse to iron to ward off evil spirits, and with the awe with which the primitive smith's craft was regarded, went a fear of the magic metal and an avoidance of it, especially in traditional and sacred ceremonies.

Possibly there is an element of priestly conservatism in some of the prohibitions. In the building of Solomon's temple, while there is no suggestion that metal could not be used in working the stones at the quarry, "there was neither hammer nor axe nor any tool of iron heard in the house while it was building".[3] The Pons Sublicius at Rome, which seems to have had some sacred character attached to it, had, too, to be built without metal, and fastened together with wooden pins.[4]

Roman and Sabine priests might not be shaved with iron but only with bronze razors or shears; and whenever an iron graving tool was brought into the sacred grove of the Arval

---

[1] *Kilimanjaro and its People* (Dundas). A special power, too, dwells in their hammers.
[2] *Vanishing Tribes in Kenya* (Major Browne).
[3] 1 Kings vi, 7.
[4] *Vide* the author's *Story of the Bridge*.

Brothers at Rome for the purpose of cutting an inscription in stone, an expiatory sacrifice had to be made, which was repeated when the tool was removed from the grove. Generally, iron might not be brought into Greek sanctuaries. The Archon of Plataea might not touch iron, except that once a year, at the commemoration of the men who fell at the battle of Plataea, he could carry a sword with which to sacrifice a bull.[1]

In many cases, metal was taboo altogether in religious ceremonies and sacrifices and the flint knife of a far older civilization was retained; this was so among the Hottentots of the Old World, and many of the Indian races of the New, including the ancient priesthood of Mexico.

Priestly conservatism, however, plays no apparent part in the unmistakably pagan Bale fires, and in Wales these were lit by wood friction, while the nine men who collected the wood fuel had to *divest themselves of money and metal*. The primitive Baduwis of Java would use no iron tools in tilling their fields, and even in Poland, the first introduction of iron ploughshares having been followed by bad harvests, the farmers blamed the iron and went back to wood.[2] In Corea, the sovereign's person was hedged with a divinity that had an antipathy to iron, and metal might not ever touch the august body; rather than have an abscess lanced with a steel instrument, King Cheng-jong, in 1800, died from the effects of the disease.[3]

Contrasting with all this is the belief of the Lakhers of Thibet that iron is a symbol of strength, and, when a man takes over a new house, the oldest member of the family proffers a hoe, of which each member takes hold and is led by it into the house.[4]

[1] *The Golden Bough* (Frazer).
[2] Ibid.
[3] *Corea, the Hermit Nation* (W. E. Griffis).
[4] *The Lakhers* (Parry).

CHAPTER IV

SMITH CLANS AND CASTES

The smith also sitting by the anvil, and considering the iron work, the vapour of the fire wasteth his flesh, and he fighteth with the heat of the furnace: the noise of the hammer and the anvil is ever in his ears, and his eyes look still upon the pattern of the thing that he maketh; he setteth his mind to finish his work, and watcheth to polish it perfectly.

So doth the potter . . .

All these trust to their hands: and every one is wise in his work. Without these cannot a city be inhabited: and they shall not dwell where they will, nor go up and down. They shall not be sought for in public counsel, nor sit high in the congregation: they shall not sit on the judges' seat nor understand the sentence of judgment: they cannot declare justice and judgment; and they shall not be found where parables are spoken.

But they will maintain the state of the world, and their desire is in the work of their craft.

Ecclesiasticus 38, v, 28–34.

DESPITE the importance of metal working and the indispensability of the craftsman, the manual worker was generally a despised or "low-caste" being throughout the ancient East, and has remained so in most parts. In India, practically all forms of manual labour fall into the lowest of the four main divisions of society and rank after the Sudras or cultivators. In Malabar, blacksmiths pollute a Brahman at twenty-four feet distance.[1] In Arabia, though smiths are attached to most communities, they are a despised class. The Tuareg tribesmen not only look down upon blacksmiths, but, since they live by fire, they believe them to be destined for Hell!

To a large extent of course this attitude is the result of a contempt for manual work on the part of landowners, warriors, and the like, and no doubt, in the case of the blacksmiths, the

---

[1] *The Land of the Lingam* (Miles, 1933).

Doorway, St. Saviour, Dartmouth. (The ironwork is certainly earlier than the date on the door)

Norman doorway and ironwork, Barfreston Church, Kent

nature of their work arouses some sense of repugnance among the more "finicky" people of the community.

There is, however, another significant side to this phase. In an astonishing number of cases, the smiths of a nation are of a different race, or a different section of the race, from those for whom they are working.[1] No doubt the segregation of the craft is, as in the case of the old-time witch, largely the creation of its practitioners themselves, through the turning of their profession into a closely guarded "mystery", and the handing down of trade secrets through the family from age to age. This, normally, should create an exclusive community or an aristocracy of craftsmanship, and in some cases, as in the instance of the ancient Celts, it did. The Lambas of Northern Rhodesia held smiths in great esteem, and a great number of their chiefs learnt the trade. Among them, too, Dr. Doke says there are evident remains of a guild of smiths. The chief of the Fan tribe, West Africa, is a smith: the smiths' craft is sacred and none but a chief may meddle with it.[2]

With the Kushites, occupying North African territory in the first millennium A.D., a smith was a noble, and fit to be a king's son. The town of Awka, in Nigeria, was the headquarters of the Nri guild of blacksmiths, a band of men of high prestige, not only as craftsmen, but also as priests owning an oracle. The Ayaka society was founded by such smiths and they had a sacred tree, into which nails—no doubt provided by the smiths for a consideration—were driven by supplicants.[3] The Ogboni society of Nigeria, too, was originally in the hands of the blacksmith clan.

All over the world, the smith's trade has been largely, either by the operation of the caste system, by the possession of trade secrets, or by circumstance, hereditary. Smithing among many African races, as in the case of the Wachagga, is confined to certain clans or societies to which admission may only be obtained, other than by blood, on payment of a fee. In most cases the blacksmith is regarded with awe, if not with esteem. The Bantu people of the Lake Nyasa area fear as well as honour him. He is "joked about as much as the plumber with

[1] The Foula smiths of West Africa are said to be almost all descended from captives.
[2] The Golden Bough (Frazer).
[3] West African Secret Societies (Butt-Thomson).

C

us", with sayings such as "as great a thief as the blacksmith", "as big a liar as the blacksmith", "the blacksmith gets rich out of other people's property", just as any successful worker in Europe often is. These things are not uttered in his presence, though, for he is in touch with mysterious powers and his ancestors are potent.[1]

Boy initiates of the Bushongo (Belgian Congo) have to creep through a tunnel having four niches, each hiding a source of terror; the first is a man disguised as a leopard, the second a warrior with a knife, the fourth a man with an ape's mask, and armed with a knife; the third is a smith, with furnace and red-hot irons.

There is an occasional touch of actual ostracism in Africa. An Elgeyo smith may not marry outside his class, since, if he married a woman not in his class, her brother would soon die! Blacksmiths are despised among the Masai; the craft is inherited, the son first practising it after marriage, and the first smith having been an immigrant who married a Masai girl. No doubt this alien origin is the real reason for the antagonism, but the one given is that they were cursed and made eternally impure and supernaturally dangerous because they make weapons and God dislikes bloodshed.[2] Yet the Masai themselves are a race of warriors! So, too, the Mashona smiths are a class apart, and regarded with awe mixed with disdain. The Tomal, the hereditary blacksmith clan of Somaliland, are of low caste.

The usual position of the smith in black Africa, however, is one of high repute, and this is perhaps the logical status in a primitive society so much dependent on his skill and knowledge of metal working, just as it should have been among prehistoric men, to most of whom the craft would be a high mystery, a gift of the gods, or something akin to sorcery. Indeed, the African smith, as in the case of the Chuka, is often credited with magic power.

In the Eastern world, except in the case of aboriginal races, the status of the smith is markedly different. There are several reasons for this, but the basic one seems to be that the smiths are generally not merely of a separate clan, but actually of a different race. Their possession of a mystery makes them

---

[1] *The Spirit-Ridden Konde* (Mackenzie, 1925).
[2] *Mining and Metallurgy in Negro Africa* (Cline).

valuable and to some extent feared. There are only two things
to do with people who are feared, in superstitious societies—
pay homage to them or keep them under; a policy that one
feels is not always absent in more advanced societies too! Then
again, in uneducated society there is always the distrust of the
foreigner, especially the foreigner whose ways are not ours.

The relationship between Eastern folk and their alien smiths
is graphically portrayed in Pierre Olivier Lapie's book, *My
Travels Through Chad*. The Haddad, blacksmiths, weavers,
potters and doctors, but especially blacksmiths, a separate tribe
from the Arabic peoples around them, "whom centuries of
bullying had made distrustful", but who, no doubt, were also
from the beginning jealous of their "mystery", keep to themselves and are accused by their more orthodox neighbours of
being still infidels at heart, carrying on unorthodox practices,
in spite of their supposed conversion to Islam. One reason,
indeed, given for the antagonism of the Moslems to the smiths
is that a blacksmith betrayed the Prophet to his enemies and
was cursed by him. There is a marked analogy here to the
position of the gypsies, whose nominal Christianity is still half
pagan and suspect, and who were, not very long ago, regarded
as heathens in many parts of Europe. Like the gypsies, too,
there are legends woven around them. The Prophet himself is
supposed to have endeavoured, without success, to convert
them, with the result that they sought refuge south-westwards,
passing through the Nile valley and on to Nigeria. They are
said to have arrived in the Wadai district of Chad about the
fifteenth century A.D., and to have been converted by Abd-el-
Krim in the following century, no doubt more or less forcibly
and with reservations which account for their suspected
paganism at heart.

Another legend told among the Haddad themselves relates
how, when Adam left the earthly paradise, he and his offspring
wandered in the country of Cham, suffering grievously, until
God, taking pity on them, sent them an angel to furnish them
with the instruments they needed. Calling together the children
of Adam, the angel made an axe, a spade, a knife and a needle
—all, be it observed, the implements of peace and cultivation.
But the sons of Adam, growing bold, demanded to be shown
how to protect themselves against their enemies, so Sulyman,

the son of the angel, made the iron malleable like wet clay, and
with his divine hands forged a helmet, a cuirass and a sword.
The men then understood that iron was a gift of God and that
they could make of it tools for working and weapons for hunting and fighting; when they knew how to work the iron, the
angel, Mahamat, called the Riguebets, in the wadi near Medina,
blacksmiths. Thus, again, the mysterious new craft is given
a divine origin.

The legendary account of the Haddad goes on:

"When Moussa went up the mountain to speak face to
face with God, he took with him the chief of the blacksmiths,
Lalouale. God then dictated the Law and Lalouale wrote it
down on brazen tablets. He also wrote down in a book of
iron pages the method of working metals."

This book he gave to the blacksmiths, all of whom are
descended from Lalouale, but the sons of the blacksmith of
Moses lost the book. "They rewrote it imperfectly from memory
on thin parchment, and that is why the blacksmiths of today
are ignorant of the processes of their forefathers." "This is the
story the fakirs tell when they speak of the Haddads—a strange
race who alone know the mysteries of iron and fire."[1]

Stripped of all imaginative and legendary embellishments,
the plain fact emerges that the smiths here are a separate race
who possessed the secret of ironworking before their neighbours
and have held both themselves and their craft aloof, or have
been left to practise it as being a despised occupation, despite
the power the knowledge gave them. There is a distinct suggestion, too, of gypsy relationship, in their paganism, their
segregation, and their migrations. Doughty, indeed, speaks of
the Solubba of Arabia as a primitive gypsy tribe of tinkers and
arms smiths, who do not keep cattle, are very poor and despised,
and molested by none.[2] There is a link there with the position
of the Chagga smiths of East Africa, who, though now held in
high esteem, may once have been regarded as outcasts and
unclean, as with smiths among the warlike Masai; smiths there
are never killed or taken captive in war.[3]

[1] *My Travels Through Chad* (P. O. Lapie).
[2] *Arabia Deserta.*
[3] *Kilimanjaro and its People* (Dundas).

This last dispensation is contrary to the Bible accounts of the dealings of Nebuchadrezzar and the Philistines with the smiths of the Israelites. When the Babylonian conqueror carried away the princes and the mighty men of valour from Jerusalem,[1] he also took all the craftsmen and smiths, and "none remained save the poorest sort of the people of the land". The Philistines, too, deprived the land of smiths, but the Israelites sharpened their shares, coulters, adzes, mattocks, though they had no spears or swords—just as the Russians, opposing Napoleon, sharpened their stove rakes as weapons. "Behold," says Isaiah, "I have created the smith that bloweth the coals in the fire and that brought forth an instrument for his work, and I have created a waster to destroy." The tools of peace have been turned into weapons more often than the sword has been beaten into a ploughshare.

No doubt the smiths, in both cases, became serf-craftsmen to their conquerors, in exile. Jews in North Africa are metal workers to their Moslem neighbours today. There seems, however, despite the Haddad legend of Moses, no evidence that the smiths of the Hebrews were an alien race, or even an inferior caste. The references in the Bible to the Babylonian captivity suggest, indeed, that the artisans were people of some importance; on the other hand, the reference in Ecclesiasticus quoted at the head of this chapter shows clearly that they were kept in their place, and could not be amongst the rulers of the people.

Further east, it is different. In the Karakoram, to the north of India, though there is little caste in the strict sense, the Bericho community of smiths are looked upon by the Hunza people as foreigners and inferiors. Here, too, the gypsy analogy applies, and it seems significant that the Bericho have a language of their own with gypsy affinities.[2]

In other cases, it does not seem to be so much a case of alien craftsmen or a despised caste of manual workers, as in India, as of a family and its descendants or a branch of a race holding in exclusive or expert knowledge. There are very few smiths among the Sema Nagas, but among the Angami Nagas blacksmithing is the most important industry after cultivation, and

---

[1] 2 Kings xxiv, 14; also Jeremiah xxix, 2.
[2] *Language Hunting in the Karakoram* (E. O. Lorimer).

there are two, three or more smiths in most villages[1]; sometimes they are cultivators as well, unlike most artisans in primitive life. Burmese Shans do not normally work in iron, but Yunnanese Shans, who know how to do blacksmith work, come in the dry season into Burmese territory, where they set up rude anvils and outdoor furnaces. There they produce hoes, mend ploughs, or make new coulters.[2]

No doubt the ironworkers were exclusive groups in prehistoric times. Evidence of ironworking is often concentrated, as in the case of the Iron Age fields in Fogstrup Hede, Denmark, where a small valley running through the area is called "Smeddal", smith-dale.[3] Certain ancient races in Asia Minor, legendary or otherwise, were famous as ironworkers, and their names probably represent hereditary clans of smiths, to whom mythical origins have been ascribed.

---

[1] *The Sema Nagas*, and *The Angami Nagas* (Hutton).
[2] *The Shans at Home* (Milne and Cochrane).
[3] *Antiquity*, Vol. XII, 149.

CHAPTER V

HEPHAESTUS, THE SMITH-GOD

> I never associate Vulcan and his Cyclops with the idea
> of a forge. These gentry would be the very last people in
> the world to flit across my mind whilst gazing at the
> forge from the bottom of the dark lane . . . they are highly
> unpoetical fellows, as well they may be, connected as they
> are with Grecian mythology. At the very mention of their
> names, the forge burns dull and dim, as if snowballs had
> been suddenly flung into it.
>
> GEORGE BORROW: *Lavengro*.

THE marvellous and mysterious properties of iron, the
knowledge involved in its extraction from the ore, and the skill
in its working, necessarily endowed it, in simple minds, with
a divine connection, evidenced, in primitive societies permeated
with animistic beliefs, in the deification of the metal or the
forge. With the personification of the divine attributes, the
smith-god becomes almost as inevitable as the god of fire, with
whom, indeed, he is often identified, as in the case of the
Circassian fire-god, Tleps, who is also the patron of metal
workers. If Agni is a god of fire alone, it is because he is perhaps
the oldest of the fire-gods, personified before the age of the
smith. The present lowly state of the Indian blacksmiths would
not in itself preclude the belief in a smith-god.

In Homeric Greece, handicraftmen were not despised, and
even later several well-known families in Athens were celebrated
for the manufacture of metal implements. The father of Demos-
thenes had a reputation for knives, and Lysias was famous for
his shields. Xanthus the smith was so proud of his trade that
he caused it to be inscribed on his statue that he was born of
iron.[1] Neither in the Iliad nor in the Odyssey is there a skilled
craftsman who is a slave, but goldsmiths, as in other parts and
ages, were the most noted and honoured among metal workers.[2]
In later Greek times, however, handicraftmen were certainly

---

[1] Fosbroke's *Encyclopaedia of Antiquities*.
[2] *The Master Craftsmen* (Gompertz).

looked down upon. In vain, law-givers, in their wisdom, tried to impress the citizens with the importance of handicrafts and the honourable nature of the craftsman's occupation, and in vain democrats gave political equality to the artisans; there was even a law prohibiting anybody from publicly reproaching a citizen with his occupation.

Artists, whose work depended on handicrafts, and who, with few exceptions, worked for pay, were put in the same class with shoemakers, bakers and smiths,[1] themselves artists all in their way. It was to a large extent an old version of the segregation of the professionals from the amateurs. Agriculture alone was allowable as fit for a respectable Greek—yet, more than anything, it was dependent on the blacksmith. Aristotle regarded most forms of manual labour as unbecoming a free Greek, Xenophon praised agriculture but condemned handicrafts, and Cicero later opined that trade and handicrafts are beneath the dignity of a free Roman citizen.

Nevertheless, even in India the Moondahs had their blacksmith gods,[2] and the Greeks an elaborate mythology based upon the forge.

The central figure in the Greek mythology of metal working is the god Hephaestus. He, too, was a god of fire. The Greek myths made him a son of Zeus and Hera, but so disliked by his mother that she threw him out of Olympus. On another occasion, having offended Zeus, he was again thrown out, falling for a whole day and landing on the island of Lemnos. Legend makes him lame—either from birth or through the fall; it is probable that this physical deformity was thrust upon the mythological conception on account of his occupation as a smith. Just as musicians and poets are believed sometimes to have developed their gifts by reason of infirmity, so it is probable that men who were actually physically strong but precluded from being efficient warriors by reason of lameness became instead artisans in a craft which required strength but not general mobility; in other words, as Gompertz puts it, their strength of arm and fine trunk development compensated for faulty legs, in the capacity of ironworkers, as they would not in many other elementary occupations.

[1] *Home Life of the Ancient Greeks* (Zimmern).
[2] *Primitive Folk* (Reclus).

Legend also links Hephaestus in marriage either with Aphrodite, goddess of love, or with Charis, one of the Graces. In the former case there is an ancient Aryan explanation. Agni, Hindu god of fire, was god of love too; such an association of fire and emotion appealed to the ancients, and occurs again in the combined rôle of Brigit, the Celtic goddess of fire and poesy. In Greek mythology, the divinity of love was separate and female, in the person of Aphrodite: what more natural then than to join her in marriage with the god of fire and so preserve the connection? His alternative spouse, Chalcis, seems to mark a later conception, arising from the association of art in metal working, Hephaestus himself appearing as a producer of artistic works, especially in the precious metals. He it was who made the beautiful Pandora, who let loose the boxed-up evils on the world; true, he is said to have made her in clay, but that would probably have been the initial process, anyway, if she was eventually created in gold. The Finnish smith-god Ilmarinen, too, made a golden woman. Chalcis is, however, primarily a goddess of spring, and in this connection there is a link with the fertility cult everywhere associated with fire.

As with most of the early smiths, Hephaestus was not merely described as a blacksmith, but as a worker in all metals. When the gods equipped Hercules, Hephaestus provided trappings of gold, and Athene gave him a great iron rattle that Hephaestus had made. He gave a beautiful necklace and veil to Cadmus and Harmonia on their marriage, and made Talos, an iron watchman, for Minos, King of Crete, as well as images of golden handmaids to serve himself. He made a golden dog, the famous armour of Achilles and Aeneas, and the fire-breathing bulls of Aetes which guarded the golden fleece. In the Iliad, xviii, 477 *et seq.*, he fashioned a shield:

"And the bellows, twenty in all, blew on the crucibles, sending deft blasts on every side, now to aid his labour and now anon howsoever Hephaestus willed, and the work went on. And he threw bronze that weareth not into the fire and tin and precious gold and silver, and next he set on an anvil stand a great anvil, and took in his hand a sturdy hammer, and in the other he took the tongs. First fashioned he a

shield, great and strong, adorning it all over, and set thereto
a shining rim, triple, bright glancing and therefrom a silver
baldrick."

In Crete, he was the inventor of iron forging, honoured by
the metal workers. Diodorus Siculus makes him the inventor of
all work in iron, copper, gold and silver, and in all substances
wrought by means of fire. This, again, suggests the identity of
the smith-god with the fire-god. At Athens, he was associated
with Athene and Prometheus—with Athene as joint givers of
civilization to Athens, with Prometheus because Prometheus
brought the gift of fire, hitherto, as elsewhere, the prerogative
of the gods, to man. Hephaestus indeed made the chains with
which Prometheus was bound for his sacrilege, but the legends
make him do so unwillingly. Torch races were held in honour of
the gods, which can but be an allusion to the way in which
Prometheus brought the fire.

Usually, Hephaestus is represented as a heavily built and
middle-aged man with a beard, holding a hammer, and sometimes the smith's pincers or tongs as well—he is typical of the
artisan of classical Greece.

Hephaestus, however, unlike the Celtic or Teutonic smith-
gods, was not a solitary worker. Rather, like Tubal-Cain, he
was the master-craftsman. Myths of Asia Minor tell of Dactyli,
Cabiri, Corybantes, Curetes, and Telchines, who were celebrated
metallurgists. In the ordered theocracy of ancient Greece,
however, Hephaestus' assistants were the Cyclops, the beings
who made the thunderbolts of Jove (Zeus). They, too, are genii
of the fire as well as the forge. Masks of satyrs and grotesques
on braziers, which were said to have been put there to avert
evil influences from the food being cooked, have been identified, as with similar masks attached to forges and ovens on
the painted vases, as those of the attendant workmen of
Hephaestus.

There is a distinct suggestion of the diffusion of ironworking
in the classical world, as well as a popular connection with the
mysterious forces of nature, in the localities in which Hephaestus set up his workships. First of all, he worked among the gods,
on Olympus; it was there that he made the golden females to

serve him. From thence he went to Lemnos, where the Cyclops
appear as his workmen, and then to Mount Etna and the
Lipari islands.

"In Lipara and Strongyle (these are some of the islands
of Aeolus) Hephaestus is thought to dwell. Hence here can
be heard the thunder of fire and violent noise. Of old it was
said that any man who would bring unworked iron could
call the next morning and take away the sword or what
else he had ordered, provided he put down the proper fee."[1]

There is also a reference to the sea boiling, which presents
a picture of Stromboli in the present age.

Working in the bowels of volcanoes, he and his assistants
became gods of the underworld instead of the sky. Was this
perhaps because he had become, instead of the goldsmith-artist
he was before the advent of the coarser metal, predominantly
an ironworker—a blacksmith?

In the quotation at the head of this chapter one detects
some prejudice on Borrow's part against the classical world.
At the same time, it is not difficult to realize what he means.
Like the gods of Olympus in general, Hephaestus and his
Roman counterpart, Vulcan, are sophisticated and bear little
relationship to the humble, honest craftsman of the village
forge. Yet he, too, was in ancient Greece. Most of the skilled
craftsmen there had no fixed workshops, but visited their
clients. Even the goldsmith "came holding in his hands his
tools, the instruments of his craft, anvil and hammer and
well-made pincers" (Odyssey, III, 434 et seq.). Every village,
however, had its forge, "where the neighbours came to
gossip in winter and where beggars were allowed to enjoy
the residual warmth during the night".[2] Rural life is far
more unchanging than urban, because it is closer to nature.
The tools of the Greek and Roman smiths, too, were much
the same as those of the modern village smithy. In the
representation of a smithy on a Greek vase, a young workman crouches near the hearth, holding a piece of iron on the

[1] From the lost treatise of Pytheas of Marseilles, quoted in *Antiquity*,
Vol. VII, p. 66.
[2] *The Master Craftsmen* (Gompertz).

anvil with the forceps in his right hand, while another workman, also unclothed, strikes the iron with a massive two-handed hammer. Two men, possibly customers, are seated on low stools, and on the walls hang hammers, chisels, drills and other tools, as well as products such as a sword and a can.[1]

The tools of Hephaestus are given as bellows of three sorts, crucibles, tongs, anvils, hammers, hammers sharp at one end, chafing dishes, whetstones, forges—and over them a prophylactic against envy—a phallus hung round with bells. The classical smith made tools, fellies and naves of wheels, pegs, keys, bars, bolts, chains, pestles, door pivots, door rings, bars for fastening doors, etc.,[2] as well as the more spectacular productions already mentioned. A hoard of blacksmiths' tools from Silchester, in the Reading Museum, includes tongs, wedges, rough iron bars, striking hammers, a T-shaped iron anvil and other implements, as well as a plough coulter with a small blade, and miniature anvils used for sharpening scythes in the field.

The anvil, with the hammer and tongs, was supposed to have been invented by Kinyras of Cyprus.[3] According to

Vulcan: plaque from Barkway, Herts (by permission of the British Museum)

pictorial representations and to actual finds, the anvil varied in form; it consisted either of one block, or three blocks superimposed on one another, or of a wooden base on which the iron anvil proper rested, in the last case being fastened into the base by means of a long point. It was either square or circular in cross-section, either hollowed out conically or made in the shape of a long horn. The classical smith usually appears bearded, but his assistants clean-shaven; often he is shown doing his work in a sitting position—probably only when he was forging the smaller objects.

[1] *Home Life of the Ancient Greeks* (Zimmern).
[2] Fosbroke's *Encyclopaedia of Antiquities.*
[3] Neuburger, *Technical Arts of the Ancients.*

Vulcan, the Roman version of Hephaestus, who takes over the business, so to speak, including the staff of one-eyed Cyclops, is, from the outset, a smith, concerned at first almost entirely with the production of arms and only later with industrial ironwork. He has not the legendary appeal of Hephaestus, his artistry and his romance. But he is still the god of fire, and as such is depicted as having been puny at birth, since the great and potent flame develops from the tiny spark. He, too, is the patron-divinity of all artisans, but especially of the smiths.

CHAPTER VI

WAYLAND, THE HERO-SMITH

> The strangest and most entertaining life ever written,
> that of a blacksmith in the olden North, Volundr or
> Velunt, who lived in woods and thickets and made keen
> swords, so that when placed in a running stream they
> would divide an object borne against them by the water
> —he married a king's daughter and had a son a bold
> knight.
>
> GEORGE BORROW: *Lavengro.*

LOGICALLY, Thor, the god of the hammer, should be the
counterpart of Hephaestus and Vulcan in Norse mythology, but
though his hammer is both emblem and main weapon, and
though one of his wives was Iarnsaxa (iron stone), he seems to
have little active association with the forge. The first smiths,
indeed, are described as dwarfs, just as Hephaestus, though
powerful, was lame. When Loki was forced to make amends
for his cutting off the hair of Sif, Thor's second wife, it was to
the dwarf Dvalin he went for the golden thread and for gifts to
Odin and Frey, a commission so well executed that he declared
the artificer to be the "most clever of smiths", a challenge
taken up by the dwarf Brock, on behalf of his brother Sindri,
who, he claimed, would produce three objects which would
surpass Dvalin's, not only in value but in magical properties—
the primitive association of metals with magic again.

Sindri set to work, with Brock blowing the bellows, and
Loki, having transformed himself into a gadfly, striving to
interrupt the work. Once again there is the suggestion of gold
being the first and iron the last of the metals to come to the
forge; first Sindri turned out a golden-haired boar, then the
magic ring, Draupnir, from which eight similar rings dropped
every ninth night, and finally the iron hammer, Miolnir, which,
despite a short handle due to Loki's attentions having drawn
blood and temporarily blinded the smith, became the wonderful
hammer of Thor.

In Thor's fight with the giant Hrungnir, we see the allegorical representation of the struggle between the new race, possessed of iron, and the old barbaric peoples of the later Stone Age, for Hrungnir's club and shield were of flint, and Thor's hammer of iron shattered the stone club, so emphasizing the superiority of modern weapons and the magic of the smith's craft.

The dwarf dwellers in the caves of the mountains, no doubt early miners and metal workers really existing and possibly actually stunted in growth, were artificers of versatility, working in any metal and in gems as well. They even made the slight-looking but magically strong rope of "silk" which finally bound Fenris, the evil wolf. Probably, one thinks, the "silken" rope was a fine steel chain. There was still no real god-smith. The divinity which hedged a mythical metal worker, however, could not fail to creep into the story of the Teutonic smith, and so we have Wayland, or Volund, the hero-smith of Norse mythology, German tradition and Anglo-Saxon legend.

According to the northern myths, Volund was one of three brothers who came upon three of the Valkyries bathing and induced them to remain on earth and become their wives. After eight years, however, the Valkyries, pining for their old abode, disappeared, and Volund's two brothers set out on a fruitless quest to find their beloved. Volund remained at home, hoping, and making rings in imitation of one his wife had given him. It is notable that, here again, Volund the smith is a worker in silver and gold as well as in iron. One night, he was surprised in his sleep and carried off by the king of Sweden, who took possession of the magic sword Mimung, which Volund had made and retained for his own use, as well as the golden love-ring.[1] Volund himself was put on an island and hamstrung to prevent his escape—so once more the smith is lame. Here he was compelled to forge weapons and ornaments for the king's use, as well as a labyrinth.

In the details of this fable, one gets the position of the smith as a highly skilled and valuable master of a mysterious craft, the making of a serf-smith in subservience to the warrior, and the versatility of the early artificer. Even that far-flung

[1] According to one version, Wieland or Volund came to the court of the king, and there defeated in fight the smith Amilias.

descendant from the forge, the aeroplane, is forecast, as Volund
proceeds to plan escape with the aid of a pair of wings that he
made. Having got the magic sword again into his hands for the
purpose of repairing it, he substituted another, and, enticing
the king's sons into the smithy, slew them. Again the artist
emerges, dovetailed into the barbarian. He fashioned drinking
vessels from the skulls of the slain and from their eyes and teeth,
which he gave as presents to the lads' unsuspecting parents and
sister.[1] One does not see much of Borrow's idealized Wayland
there!

> But their skulls,
> Beneath their hair,
> He in silver set,
> And to Nidud gave,
> And of their eyes
> Precious stones he formed.
>
> (Lay of Volund)

Then Bodvild, the sister, possessed of the love-ring, brought
it to the smithy to be repaired. She he drugged and seduced,
then rose upon the wings he had made, carrying the magic
sword and ring, and declaring that the former would eventually
be given to Sigmund—as the myth relates duly happened.

At Alf-heim, among the immortals, Volund then took up
his abode, reunited to his wife, and translated into a demi-god.[2]
Still he remained the smith, making suits of impenetrable
armour, such as the one Beowulf wore, and magic swords,
including Mimung, Flamberge, the sword of Aymon and his
son Renaud, and Joyeuse, the sword of Charlemagne. Norse
legend avers that the first sword was forged by Volund or
Wayland for Odin. Of another of his swords, an Anglo-Saxon
poem runs:

> It is the mate of Miming,
> Of all swerds it is king,
> And Weland it wrought,
> Bitterfer it is hight.

[1] A casket, in carved ivory, of Northumbrian workmanship of the eighth
century A.D. or so, fragments of which are in the possession of the British
Museum, shows Volund holding the skull of one of the boys with the usual
smith's tongs, and hammers are also represented.
[2] *Myths of the Norsemen* (Guerber).

Works of a mediaeval clock, Salisbury Cathedral

Such, in brief, was the story of Volund, Wayland, or Vieland. In England, he was Wayland, the wonderful smith. Anglo-Saxon tradition makes him the son of a sailor-hero, Vade or Wate, and a mermaid: he was also said to be the grandson of a king of Norway. He makes a magic boat, a winged garment, famous swords, helmets and armour. In English folklore attached to the long barrow in Berkshire called "Wayland Smith's Cave", he would magically shoe a horse if corn was left under his stone, or a sixpence, overnight, just as Vulcan would make the desired article in the time. The farrier Wayland, though, sounds like a mediaeval adaptation, and the sixpence a later corruption still. Geoffrey of Monmouth makes him a worker in the precious metals, as he was in Norse mythology.

The "Galland" of the French romances is invariably a magic swordsmith. The variations epitomize the story of the smith—first the worker in all metals, goldsmith and blacksmith too, then the armourer-smith, the skilled craftsman of early mediaeval romance, and then the village smith-farrier of countryside folklore.

Sigurd, son of Sigmund, and popular hero of Teutonic myth more generally known as Siegfried, had Regin, the king's smith, for his foster-father, and Regin again is of the race of the dwarfs. The Aesir trio, Odin, Thor and Loki, again wandering on earth, slay Regin's brother Otter and have to fill the skin with gold as an atonement; again the gold worker whom they rob for the ransom is a dwarf. Sigurd himself learnt the smith's craft, the art of carving runes, languages, music and eloquence, but, unlike his teacher, he became a warrior too. Regin, cheated by Loki and Fafnir of the gold of atonement, took refuge among men, teaching them to work metals and practically every civilized craft—one more tribute to the reiterated versatility of the early artisan.

In Scandinavia, the hero-smiths and the divine character of Volund raised the blacksmith's art to a respectable position, far more so than did the classical Hephaestus or Vulcan, nor did it lose caste on the introduction of Christianity. Of a ceremonial and unusable whetstone found in the Sutton Hoo ship burial, Sir Thomas Kendrick writes:

D

"It is a unique savage thing and inexplicable, except perhaps as a symbol, proper to the king himself, of the divinity and mystery which surrounded the smith and his tools in the heathen world."

But the smith is still the artisan, not the god. So, too though folklore stories of Scandinavia may be dressed in the setting of Christian days, they still remain the pagan stories of the conflict with Troll and Giant, figuring sometimes as the Devil of Christian theology. The wandering Aegir become our Lord and St. Peter in the tale of the Master Smith, who made a bargain with the Devil—but it is the hammer, the hammer of Thor, which the smith eventually uses on the Devil, not the tongs of St. Dunstan. So also is it the hammer in "The Lad and the De'il".

Saxon smithy. From an ancient manuscript

CHAPTER VII

THE MAGIC SWORD

The first artificer of death, the shrewd
Contriver who first sweated at the forge
And forg'd the blunt and yet unblooded steel
To a keen edge and made it bright for war
And the first smith was the first murd'rer's son.

COWPER: *The Task*

N NORTHERN legend and tradition, the sword was indubitbly the masterpiece of the blacksmith's art. Even in the day f bronze weapons, Merenptah, Egyptian Pharaoh, had been iven a sword by his god, Ptah, but it was the advent of iron-working that made the sword the prized weapon of the doughty arrior. In Norse mythology, the initial appearance of the forge i in connection with the building of the palaces of the gods, ιade of precious metals. The first period of their habitation as the "Golden Age", an imaginary period of peace and appiness, the name of which fitly symbolizes the order in hich the metals were worked. To the Golden Age, in old elief, succeeded the "brass" age—the age of craft, commerce nd strife, the age of bronze weapons, limited in their production nd efficiency. Then came the Iron Age, "when war began"; on swords and spearheads were cheaper, more deadly and ιore readily come by than those of bronze. An address of the honds of India to the god of war, indeed, accuses black-niths, among others, of inciting him to send them to war for ιeir profit.[1] Once again a familiar plaint echoes down the ages, ιough the blacksmith has become the armament manufacturer.

Some archaeologists believe that the so-called "currency ιrs" of the Early Iron Age were rough forgings, ready to be nished off into swords by the skilled smith, or the two opera-ons, "mooding" and "smithing", might have been carried out y the same worker, on the same anvil, without being con-nuous. The final process would have been the grinding to an

[1] *Primitive Folk* (Reclus).

edge. The sword of the Halstatt, or first iron, period closely resembled bronze swords, and its softness made it untrust-worthy in action. In the La Tene periods which followed, a straighter blade was evolved, and it was forged thinner. In some cases, little strips of soft iron were welded on the sides to form cutting edges.

A Lake-dwelling sword was found to be made of steel formed by hammering several strips together. Early black-smiths learned by experience that the thinner the blade was forged, the more rapidly it hardened when heated in a charcoal fire and subsequently quenched, so they hammered their edges thin, doubled and welded them together, and finally tempered them by heating and quenching.[1] All this means skill and knowledge, in varying degrees, and differences in the quality of the blades are distinguishable at an early period.

Hence, no doubt, the stories of the magic sword—the sword produced by a blacksmith of renown, a legendary and archaic Andrea Ferrara, and possessing qualities which made it superior to the common product, and, with the exaggeration of hearsay, something supernaturally endowed. Secret processes would enhance the awe with which such a sword would be surrounded. So, in the north, where the sword was paramount it even acquired some sort of sacredness, which led to oaths made on it being particularly binding, long before the cross hilt introduced the sanctity of the Christian into the matter According to Dr. J. F. Hodgetts,[2] when two northern warriors formed a bond of brotherhood, each cut a rune in his own left arm and then applied the mystic figure to the corresponding arm of his friend. The two left arms were bound together for a short time, the two swords were planted, point downwards, in the ground between them, and over the swords the right hand of each grasped the right hand of the other and brotherhood was sworn. So, too, the sword stood with its hilt towards the sky when a vassal swore fealty to the king.

Tyr, the Norse god of war, was considered the patron of the sword, so the sign or rune representing him—the head of his javelin—had to be engraved on the blade of every sword, an observance enjoined by the Edda as conducing to victory

---

[1] *Antiquity*, Vol. VII, p. 63.
[2] *Older England* (1884).

Runes of victory shalt thou know,
if thou wilt have the victory,
and cut them on thy sword-hilt,
some on the hilt rings,
some on the plates of the handle,
and twice name the name of Tyr.

Ie has been identified with the Saxon god Saxnot (sax = the hort Saxon sword) and Cheru, chief god of the Cheruski, whose word, according to an ancient legend, had been fashioned by he dwarfs, sons of Ivald, who made Odin's spear, and it ensured 'ictory to its possessor. After its disappearance from a temple, t was alleged to have been brought by a stranger to Cologne nd given to Vitellius, the Roman prefect, who, thanks to his possession of such a talisman, was elected Roman Emperor. ɔrown careless in his exalted position, he did not discover it iad been stolen until Vespasian had been named Emperor in iis stead, and was beheaded with the magic sword by the ɔerman soldier who had stolen it. Victory followed its possessor, vho, on his deathbed, refused to reveal where he had buried it. ʌttila found it by accident and reaped the reward, only to be lain by it in his bed by his wife, to avenge her father. After ɪnother disappearance, it was said to have been unearthed by he Duke of Alva, Charles V's general. The Franks held yearly nartial games in its honour, but, with the advent of Christianty and the Church's adaptation of pagan beliefs, it became the ɪttribute of the Archangel St. Michael, in whose hands it has ːver since been shown.[1] Frey, too, god of the sunshine, received rom the gods a marvellous sword which had the power of ɪghting victoriously on its own accord as soon as it was drawn rom its sheath, but in his case the sword seems to be allegorical nd represents the rays of the sun.

Another sword which fought of its own accord and could not ɪe sheathed, after it was once drawn, until it had tasted blood, ʔas the mythical sword Tyrfing, which could cut through iron nd stone; this was made by the mysterious dwarfs of Norse ɔgend and given to Angantyr. It was buried with him, as was he case with many of the trusted weapons of the Norse chiefains, but his daughter recited magic spells to compel him to ise from his grave to give to her the blade, which passed into

[1] *Myths of the Norsemen* (Guerber).

another hero's possession; losing the sword, however, he los
reason and power of speech also. "Augurvadel", which Frithio
received as part of his inheritance, was also made by the dwarfs
its hilt was of hammered gold and the blade was inscribed witl
runes which were dull until it was brandished in war, whei
they flamed "red as the comb of the fighting cock".[1]

Constantly one finds one of two things happening to thes(
famous swords, unless they are captured by an enemy—eithe:
they are buried with their owners or else they are passed on a:
precious heirlooms. The popular belief in their magic propertie:
was based on the runes cut on them, which, savouring of sorcery
were looked at askance by the Christian Church. The smith':
name would probably have been a truer guarantee of thei
quality, and many swords of the Viking period were inscribec
with it; a notable name so inscribed is "Ulfberht", whos(
productions have been found scattered over north-west Europe
The name of another smith, Ingelri, probably of the tentl
century, has been found in Norway, Sweden, France, Russia
Germany, and England (the Thames, London).[2]

In the centre of the hall of the Teutonic myth-hero, Volsung
stood an oak, which grew through the roof, spreading it:
branches above. Into that hall, during a betrothal feast, strod(
a one-eyed stranger, who, at one stroke, drove the sworc
"Gram" into the oak trunk. "Let him," said he, "of all thi:
company, bear this sword who is man enough to pull it out
I give it him and none shall say he ever bore a better blade.'
The pride of the skilled craftsman rings out there, even if hi:
words are put into the mouth of a god.

Sigmund, son of Volsung, alone could withdraw the sword
but he lost it when Volsung fell; regaining his father's kingdom
he met once more the mysterious stranger, against whom th(
sword proved unavailing and broke, for the stranger was Odii
himself. Years later, Sigurd or Siegfried, son of Sigmund, se·
to slay the dragon Fafnir, finds no new sword forged by Regin
clever as that smith is, adequate for the task, so Regin, th(
master-smith, forges a new sword from the fragments of Gram
the blade of which clove the anvil in the smithy and cut a locl
of wool borne down upon it by a running stream.

[1] *Myths of the Norsemen* (Guerber).
[2] *Antiquaries Journal*, January–April, 1951.

Three magic swords come into the Dietrich[1] cycle of hero myths. Dietrich's own sword, Nagelring, was again a production of the dwarfs and stolen from a giant; it alone could pierce the skins of the giants, and having slain a giantess with it and captured a magic helm too, Dietrich placed the sword between the two halves of the severed body, to prevent the giantess, by the magic power of steel, from reuniting herself. Eckesax, too, was the sword of a giant, Ecke, with whom Dietrich fought, winning the combat only by the aid of his faithful steed, who trampled the owner of the sword to death. Mimung, the sword of Volund himself, comes into the story; Witig or Wittich, the warrior son of Volund, carries it to try his strength against the doughty Dietrich, but Hildebrand, henchman of Dietrich, substitutes another commoner sword while Wittich sleeps; it breaks, and Wittich reproaches his father with having given him an inefficient weapon, on which Hildebrand discloses his trick and restores Mimung, with which Wittich wins the renewed combat. Realizing that the magic sword alone has given him victory over the champion, Wittich thenceforward wields the famous blade in Dietrich's service.[2]

The work of the smith looms largely in the Anglo-Saxon epic *Beowulf*. Even the timber hall of Hrothgar is girt by iron bands:

> fair dwelling of mankind—but it was made so fast
> within and eke without, by clamping bands of iron
> besmithed with cunning wit.

Beowulf himself is in mail of net, linked by the skill of Wayland the Smith:

> yet send Hygelac, pray
> If the fight takes me off, this best of war corslets,
> Most splendid of garments which covers my heart,
> Hrethel had it of yore—it is Wayland's own work.

and on his companions

> each war-byrnie shone,
> each bright iron ring, hard and linked by the smith,
> sang out in their sarks.

---

[1] Dietrich is sometimes identified with Theodoric the Goth, fifth and sixth centuries, A.D., but the identification is doubtful.

[2] *Popular Tales from the Norse* (Dasent).

His helm

> with lordly bands belted as in days long past,
> the armourer made it and wondrously wrought
> with boar-figures[1] beset it.

but there is a perfect armoury of famed swords, for

> There many a chief
> Of Beowulf's clan old heirlooms swung.

Hengest, Hunlaf's son, laid "Hildeleoma, best of swords", in his lap.

> the hammer-forged blade, with adornment bedecked,
> the sword, doughty of edges and spattered with gore,
> the boar-image cleaves which stands out on the helm.

Hrunting, another famous sword, is lent to him by Unferth for his fight with the demon's mother.

> Now Hrunting was hight that same hilted sword,
> among old heirlooms it was one of the best,
> Its blade was of iron . . .
>   . . . the relic of eld, the strange wavy sword
> So hard of its edge.

Its edge, however, failed, and he discarded it.

> Mid the war-gear he saw then a conquering blade,
> titanic and old, a sword doughty of edge,
> by fighters much prized: of weapons the pick
> and yet greater it was than any man else
> was able to take to the pastime of war;
> good and comely to view and of giants the work.

The great sword slew the monster but dissolved in her hot blood

> Then was Goldenhilt given, the giants' old work
> to the veteran prince . . . It came to be owned
> by the Lord of the Danes, the cunning smith's work.

[1] The boar was sacred to Freya, and was constantly borne as a helm crest

On his departure from the scene of his exploits on Hrothgar's behalf, Beowulf gives the man who had guarded his ship a gold-mounted sword, a treasured heirloom—which, *ipso facto*, made the guard a more honoured man!

In the last scene of Beowulf's career, his sword is "Naegling", grey in colour and old, but it parted asunder in his deadly fight with the dragon of the barrow.

Not least, there is Excalibur, "cut-steel". The body of the Arthurian legends is Celtic, but their dressing is mediaeval, and the story of the sword is Teutonic, even though we have the Skye story of the golden sword, which was never drawn against man or beast whom it did not overthrow, and which the Cailleach offered as ransom for her life to the widow's son, Finlay, the Changeling, who killed the witch and took it. Excalibur, though, was not made by smith-godlet, dwarf or giant.

> King Arthur's sword, Excalibur,
> Wrought by the lonely maiden of the Lake,
> Nine years she wrought it, sitting in the deeps
> Upon the hidden bases of the hills.
>
> (TENNYSON.)

According to the version adopted by Tennyson in his *Idylls of the King*, it mysteriously appeared from the waters of the Lake

> Graven in the oldest tongue of all this world,
> Take me . . .

but Mallory's *Morte d'Arthur* gives a full account of how Arthur won his kingship, after many doubts and delays, by being the only man who could withdraw the sword, which mysteriously appeared in a churchyard, embedded in an anvil on a square block of stone and inscribed: "Whoso pulleth out the sword of this stone and anvil is rightwise king born of all England." See how the Norse story of the Volsungs echoes there! Even Arthur himself, however, failed to draw another magic sword from the scabbard; Balin alone was able to do it, but having refused to surrender it, incurred a curse, fulfilled when he killed his own brother with it unknowingly. Then this sword, too, was put in a millstone and floated down to Camelot, where Galahad retrieved it; a tragic sword, indeed, for with it Lancelot killed his best friend, Gawain. As to Excalibur, since it could not be an heirloom, and the Christianized setting of the redressed tradition eliminated a barrow-burial, it was to be thrown back into the Lake; twice Bedivere, last attendant of the king, loth to lose such a great sword, disobeyed and hid it, but finally he had to carry out Arthur's command and return it to its magic source.

Layamon and Geoffrey of Monmouth call Arthur's sword Caliburn—best of swords forged in the Isle of Avalon and wrought, says Layamon, with magic craft. Perhaps its island origin gave rise to the story of the Lake. Arthur's byrnie, according to Layamon, was made for him by Wygar "the elvish smith"—the dwarf again: his spear, called Ron by Geoffrey, by Griffin, of the city of the wizard Merlin.

Despite the acceptance of Christianity and the ban of the Church on mystic runes, the wonderful named sword of magic power survived into the early Middle Ages. Joyeuse, the sword of Charlemagne, was ascribed to the pagan smith, Wayland or Wieland; Roland and Oliver had their wonder-swords, Durandane and Altecar, the former destroyed by Roland at his death, to prevent it from falling into the hands of the pagans. Flamberge, too, sword of Aymon, handed on to his son Renaud, was broken and thrown into the Seine when Renaud was compelled by Charlemagne to sacrifice the faithful steed Bayard.[1]

Later still come the named swords of the Cid, Tizona, his own pet sword, and Colada, won from the Moors and second only to Tizona. When the Cid died his body led the Christian army into victorious battle with the Moors, Tizona in hand, and still it accompanied him when his body lay in state in San Pedro de Cardona. There, says legend, a Jew attempted to pull the dead hero's beard, whereupon:

> Ere the beard his fingers touched,
> Lo! the silent man of death
> Grasped the hilt, drew Tizona
> Full a span from out the sheath.
>   (From an ancient Spanish ballad.)

[1] *Myths and Legends of the Middle Ages* (Guerber).

Tizona, it is said, became a heirloom of the Marquis of Falies, and bore on it two inscriptions, one "I am Tizona, made in era 1040", the other "Hail, Maria, full of grace". The northern runes may have been anathema to early Christian missionaries, but, as in other cases, the Church or its adherents obviously found it possible and politic to dress a pagan practice in a Christian guise.

.   .   .   .   .

Magic sword, impenetrable byrnie, wondrous helmet—all were the work of smiths famous for their uncanny skill. Never a word of the tools of peace, yet there was perhaps even greater magic in the spade and the plough, the graving tool, the instruments of the surgeon—all the work of the smith, too.

CHAPTER VIII

GOBHA, THE CELTIC SMITH

When Vulcan gies his bellows breath
An' ploughmen gather wi' their graith,
O rare to see thee fizz and frea'th
    I' th' luggèd coup,
Then Burnewin comes on like death
    At every champ.
Nae mercy then for airn or steel,
The brownie banie ploughman chiel
Brings hard owrelip wi' sturdy wheel
    The strong forehommer
Till block an' studdie ring and reel
    wi' dinsome clamour
              R. BURNS.

THE legendary history of smithcraft among the Celts starts, as with Tubal-Cain, with a smith who was the founder of handicrafts and artistry, and, like the Teutonic Volund or Wayland, with three brothers, in Ireland, Kian, Sawan, and Goban the smith, the last sometimes described as Gavida, one of three brothers who were chiefs of Donegal, as Goibhnean or Gobhan, or Goibnu, a smith-god who made the people of the goddess Danu invulnerable with his magic drink and forged their weapons, as well as three magic cooking spits; like other mythical and African smiths, he was a sorcerer, too, and he had a reputation as a great builder and bridge-maker. Like most of the prehistoric smiths, he wandered about the country, seeking commissions.

It happened that one of the brothers, Kian, had a magical cow, which Balor, the Formorian king, resolved to acquire. One day Kian and Sawan had come to Goban's forge to have some weapons made for them, bringing fine steel for the purpose. Kian went into the forge, leaving Sawan in charge of the cow. Balor appeared, as a small boy, and told Sawan he had overheard the other two brothers conspiring to use the fine steel for their own swords, leaving only common steel for Sawan's.

60

Enraged, and without waiting for confirmation of the story, Sawan gave the cow's halter to the "boy", who promptly carried the cow off to Tory island and left the brothers thirsting for revenge. So far the tale is one of an archaic forge, to which customers brought their own material, and of the skill of a particular smith in making fine swords. To lead up to the vengeance, we then have the common story of a princess shut up in a tower by her father to prevent her having contact with men. Kian, however, disguised as a woman, reached her and made her pregnant with three sons, whom Balor, her father, ordered to be drowned at birth. One alone, dropped by the appointed executioner, escaped with life, was found by his father, and handed over by him to the tutelage of his brother, the smith, who taught him his own trade and made him skilled in all kinds of handicraft.

The child was Lugh, the appointed redeemer of the Danaan people of Ireland, Lugh of the Long Hand. When Lugh grew up, he sought service at the royal palace of Tara, first declaring himself to be a carpenter. "We are in no need of a carpenter," said the doorkeeper, "we have an excellent one in Luchta, son of Luchad." So Lugh replied that he was a smith too, and was told that there was a master-smith there already. So also when he announced himself as a warrior, poet, harper, man of science, physician—always the place was filled. But his persistence and his versatility gained him entry and the title of All-Craftsman, Prince of All the Sciences. He produced a magic boat, a magic horse, and, of course, a magic sword, Fragarach, "The Answerer", which could cut through any mail, and ranked, in Celtic mythology, with the sword of Conary Mor which sang, and the sword of Cuchulain which spoke.

He played the decisive part in the battle in which the Danaans overthrew their predecessors, the Formorians, at Moytura, in which the craftsmen of the Danaans, Goban the smith, Credne the artificer-goldsmith and Luchta the carpenter repaired the broken weapons of the Danaans with magical speed—three blows of Goban's hammer making a spear or sword, Luchta flinging a handle which stuck on forthwith, and Credne jerking rivets, with his tongs, which flew into place of their own accord.[1]

[1] *Myths and Legends of the Celtic Race* (T. W. Rolleston).

Among the British Celts, Gobniu was Govannon, brother of Amathaon, Celtic god of husbandry, and of the enchanter Gwydion ap Don. With the help of Govannon, Amathaon made fit for agriculture the wild land of Yspaddaden Penkawr, a seemingly impossible task; in modern parlance, the agriculturalist had recourse to the smith for implements of cultivation without which it would have been impracticable to till the land.

Lug or Lugh, too, appears among the other Celtic peoples; with the Continental Celts he was a master of artistic handicrafts, a sort of Celtic Vulcan or Volund, whose works included a magic spear capable of slaying by itself. Lug is generally considered to be the sun-god and a personification of fire; as such he had affinities with Brigit, the Celtic goddess of fire and poetry, who was also a patroness of the smiths. He, too, was not only a smith but a harpist, poet and taleteller, and a champion of the gods. Other notable smiths of Irish legend are Nechen, the smith of Tara, Drinne, who made the anvil of the Daghda, and Cuilean Ceard or Culann, smith of the Ultonians and foster-father of the Irish myth-hero Cuchulain.

Cuchulain himself was given as a son of Lugh. Invited to a banquet given by Culann, he arrived late and unheralded, was attacked by Culann's fearsome guardian-hound; Cuchulain, true to heroic tradition, overcame the hitherto invincible beast and slew him, so much to Culann's distress that the youth volunteered to act as house-guard himself while he trained another hound to fill the place. Cuchulain himself does not appear as a smith, but he was the son and foster-son of great smiths, and became an even greater warrior than the son of Volund. The many hero stories of Cuchulain are said to have come down from before the seventh century A.D.

Other smiths came into the myths of Ireland. Maeldun, in his voyage, came to the island of the smithy, where there was a tremendous smithy and where a giant smith came out of the forge holding in his tongs a huge mass of glowing iron, which he cast after the voyagers and made the sea boil round it when it fell astern of the boat. In that there is an unmistakable echo of the Vulcan myths, and as there are no active volcanoes in Ireland one can but associate this element of the story with the isles of the Mediterranean, where also the sea boiled near the supernatural forge. Another adventurer, in Celtic Scotland, encountered the smithy of the twenty-seven smiths, and in a Gaelic poem, *The Lay of the Smithy*, Caolte, alias Derglas, the Thinman, challenged seven mysterious smiths.[1]

Sometimes, in later lore, the smiths encounter the fairies. One disturbed the little folk when they visited his forge at night and misfortunes followed. Another, suspecting that the fairies had substituted a changeling for his son, had to light a large and bright fire before the bed. The fairy child, he was told, would say, "What is the use of such a fire as that?" Answering at once, "You will see that presently," the smith was to throw him in the middle of it. If it was his own son he would call out to be saved—rather late in the day, one thinks! —but if not, the thing would fly through the roof. On the trial of the experiment, the changeling gave a yell and sprang through the roof where the hole was left to allow the egress of the smoke. Then the smith visited the fairy hill, where his real son worked at the forge—obviously a hereditary smith—and rescued him. The young man became the inventor of a peculiarly well-tempered sword which made the fame of father and son and no doubt gave rise to the supernatural story.[2]

Generally speaking, the status of the smiths among Celtic races was high—they associated with kings, gave banquets, as in the case of Culann, and, though manual workers, held a position of privilege; a king of Erin boasted of having a smithy on shore as well as ships at sea.[3] In the Scoto-Milesian period of ancient Ireland, though the divine aura had departed, probably because ironworking had ceased to hold so much mystery and magic, craftsmen were held in high esteem, and the brazier, smith, engraver and ringmaker had places of honour in the royal hall of the Miodhchuart at Tara and at the table of the king.[4] In Wales, the Laws of Howel Dda refer to eleven royal servants who were officers of the court by custom and usage; the ninth is the smith, and the smith was one of fourteen persons who sat on chairs in the palace. A low-class man could not become a smith *or a bard* without his lord's consent.

[1] *Waifs and Strays of Celtic Tradition*, Vol. IV, Argyllshire (Ld. Archibald Campbell).

[2] *Popular Tales of the West Highlands* (Campbell).

[3] Ibid.

[4] *Ulster Journal of Archaeology*, Vol. IX, 1861–2.

While the Celtic smiths seem to have been of the race for whom they forged, there was usually a hereditary element about the craft, as in so many primitive crafts and communities. Professor O'Curry[1] refers to a tribe of goldsmiths descended from a third century A.D. king of Munster, who held land by reason of their profession down to A.D. 530 at least. The tribe, the Cerdraighe, also furnished the bronze workers. They were not ranked among the professors of the free and liberal arts but belonged to the higher class of artisans, who included the Gobha or blacksmith, the Umhaidhe or bronze worker, and the Cerd or smith in precious metals—a division of crafts which comes with the spread of metal working and is not present in its early stages. A goldsmith named Len gave the Lakes of Killarney their ancient name—Locha Lein, the Lakes of Len, of the many hammers, who worked by the Lakes.

The Gaelic words Ceard, Ceardach, Cheardaich—craftsman, smithy, forge—enter into Clan nomenclature in Scotland. The Sinclairs of Argyllshire and the west of Scotland were known as Clann na Cearda or craftsmen, and appear to be distinct from the Sinclairs of the north.[2] Several of the clans had hereditary smith septs—the Machaes, for instance, were hereditary smiths to Campbell of Breadalbane. One of the most interesting family names in this connection is that of Gow or MacGowan, derived from the ancient Gaelic word Gobha or Gobhainn, blacksmith and armourer, in turn derived from Goban, the smith-god of Ireland. The main branch of the family, however, is said to be descended from Henry Wynd, known as "An gobh crom", immortalized by Sir Walter Scott as "Hal of the Wynd", in *The Fair Maid of Perth*. The historic facts of the famous encounter of two clans on the North Inch of Perth were that it was fought in 1396 before Robert II, and it was found that one of the clans was short of a man, having only twenty-nine instead of thirty. The smith, rather than see such a notable combat fail, volunteered to take the place of the missing man on the Macphersons' side, for a consideration. Having killed one man, he rested and contented himself with self-defence, but the Macphersons being sorely pressed, their leader offered Hal further rewards if he would continue to

[1] In *Manners and Customs of the Ancient Irish.*
[2] *The Clans and Tartans of Scotland* (Robert Bain).

fight, and, being an expert swordsman, he turned the scale. In the end, but ten men on the Macphersons' side, including the smith, were left, mostly badly wounded, but only one of the opponents, said to be the Davidsons, remained and he saved himself by throwing himself into the Tay.[1]

It is a bit of a descent, after that heroic exploit, to read the folk-tale of the Highland smith who gloried in the adventures of his apprentice as a master-thief! The true craftsman is better exemplified in the story of the smith who was offered the choice of speechless art or artless speech, and, having chosen wisely if not too well, became a skilful blacksmith, but, like many other creative artists, could not make any money.[2]

[1] *The Clans and Tartans of Scotland* (Robert Bain).
[2] *Popular Tales of the West Highlands* (Campbell).

E

CHAPTER IX

THE SMITH-SAINT

St. Dunstan:
> Waked with this musick from my silent urn,
> Your patron Dunstan comes t'attend your turn,
> Amphion and old Orpheus playing by,
> To keep our forge in tuneful harmony,
> These pontifical ornaments I wear,
> Are types of rule and order all the year.
> In these white robes none can a fault descry,
> Since all have liberty as well as I:
> Nor need you fear the shipwreck of your cause,
> Your loss of charter or the penal laws,
> Indulgence granted by your bounteous prince,
> Makes for that loss too great a recompence.
> This charm the Lernaean Hydra will reclaim;
> Your patron shall the fameless rabble tame.
> Of the proud Cham I scorn to be afear'd;
> I'll take the angry Sultan by the beard.
> Nay, should the Devil intrude among your foes—
>
> (Enter Devil)
>
> Devil: What then?
> St. Dunstan: Snap, thus, I have him by the nose!
>
> (From the *Goldsmith's Pageant*, 1687.)

DESPITE the original superstitious aversion to iron by the
priesthood of pagan times, and the taint of magic attached to
it long afterwards, there were smith-saints and smith-church-
men, as well as smith-demons and smith-sorcerers.

On the one hand, we have such legends as that of Alcester,
Warwickshire, a centre of ironworking about A.D. 700, whose
smiths, for their hardness of heart in refusing to listen to
St. Egwin and endeavouring to drown his voice by beating on
their anvils, were swallowed up by the earth.[1] Or the later
Sabbatarian story of the blacksmith at Eckford, in the Scottish
border country, who, though otherwise an exemplary working
man, persisted in blowing his bellows and hammering on his

---

[1] *English Industries of the Middle Ages* (Salzman).

66

anvil on the Sabbath, while his neighbours passed on their way
to kirk, shocked, not only by his sacrilegious conduct, but
apparently even more so by the advantage he took over them
by working seven days a week. Nemesis, however, overtook the
sinner: had it been otherwise, the story would not of course
have been recorded. One Sunday morning, as the country
folk passed on their way to kirk, the smith, in his leather
apron, was hard at work as usual; a few hours later, when
the villagers came home, both smith and smithy had utterly
disappeared, and the site of the forge had become a bog.
Nothing more was ever seen of the smith, or his wife and family,
but many years afterwards the bog was drained and a smith's
anvil came to light, thereby, of course, proving the truth of
the story—or did the discovery come first and the story
afterwards?

On the other side of the case, we have the fact that there
were smiths among the saints of old Ireland—not perhaps
surprising when we realize how many obscure Celtic saints have
turned out to be pagan godlets, and there were smiths among
the gods. In Saxon England, however, there was a law of Edgar
which commanded that every priest, "to increase knowledge,
do diligently learn some handicraft".[1] Both in Saxon England
and in the Middle Ages, the monasteries had a hand in digging
ore, smelting, and forging iron, the Cistercians, whose motto
was "To labour is to pray", being active in the north of
England in this matter.

Among the English churchmen who, following out the ideas
of King Edgar, practised a craft, was St. Dunstan, who was a
smith. He made two great bells for the church at Abingdon; his
friend Ethelwald, bishop, is said to have made two other bells
for the same place of a smaller size, and a wheel full of small
bells, gilt, to be turned round for the music at feast days. He
also displayed much art in the fabrication of a large silver table
of curious workmanship. Stigand, Bishop of Winchester, made
two images and a crucifix of gilt and placed them in the cathedral
of his diocese. One of our English kings, finding that a certain
monk was a good goldsmith, made him an abbot![2] Artisanship
and craftsmanship among the monastic fraternities was not

[1] *Older England* (Hodgetts).
[2] Ibid.

unusual, despite the employment of secular workmen, and much
of the work in and around our great abbeys and cathedrals has
been done by the brethren themselves.

St. Dunstan, however, was a smith who put the tools of his
craft to good religious use. Tempted by the Devil—in the form
of a handsome maiden, according to one version—while at work
in his forge, he seized the demon by the nose with his tongs,

St. Dunstan and the Devil
(From Hone's *Every-day Book* 1826)

previously rendered red hot especially for Satan's reception.[1]
His Diabolical Majesty roared so terribly as to split the rock
in which the forge-cave was situated into three pieces. The
incident is said, in one account, to have taken place at Mayfield,
in Sussex, and an eighteenth-century writer recorded that the
tongs reputed to have been used by St. Dunstan were still to
be seen there! The Devil, in his agony, is alleged to have
jumped to Tunbridge Wells, where he landed with such force

[1] The legend is illustrated in the fourteenth-century Luttrell Psalter and in
a window in the Bodleian Library, Oxford.

as to cause a spring to flow—and that accounts for the sulphur there!

Another St. Dunstan legend relates that one day the Devil asked the smith-saint to shoe his single hoof. St. Dunstan, recognizing his customer, tied him tightly to the wall and did the job, taking particular care to give the Devil so much pain that he yelled for mercy. The saint at last agreed to release him, on condition that he would never again enter a place where he saw a horseshoe displayed. This tale is sometimes quoted as explaining why horseshoes are said to be lucky and to act as charms against witches and the like, but the origin of the idea lies further back than the Christian era, in the days of superstitious paganism and mystified awe.

Surely these exploits should have been sufficient for St. Dunstan to have been the patron saint of smiths in general, especially in England, his native land, but, with the long-standing and still prevalent leaning of English people towards the glorification of alien genius, he was often put aside for foreign saints who were far less artisans than he was supposed to have been: St. Eloi and St. Clement. Even our national saint, however, was an alien, as though we had not perfectly good saints available, such as St. Wilfrid—or the British saint, St. Alban.

The goldsmiths alone seem to have adopted St. Dunstan as their patron saint—though, at Bodmin, the smiths' fraternity was under the joint patronage of St. Dunstan and St. Eloi. The Goldsmiths' Company of London had a St. Dunstan's Feast, the cost of which, in 1473, included eight minstrels, £2 13s. 8d., with 6s. 8d. for ten bonnets for them and 3s. 4d. for their dinner, £2 10s. for two hogsheads of wine, 6s. 6d. for a barrel of muscatel, 11s. 10d. for red wine, 17s. 4d. for four barrels of good ale, and 6s. for two barrels of ale, apparently not so good, as well as spices, bread, poultry—twelve capons at 8d. each, twelve geese at 7d. each, etc.

In the Pageant of Lord Mayor Viner's time—during the reign of Charles the Second—the London Goldsmiths had a scene or car representing the Patron of the Company, St. Dunstan,

"attired in a dress properly expressing his prelatical dignity, in a robe of fine white lawn, over which he weareth a cope

St. Eloi
(From the Luttrell Psalter, by permission of the
British Museum)

or vest of costly bright cloth of gold down to the ground, on his reverend grey head a gold mitre, set with topaz, ruby, emerald, amethyst and sapphire. In his left hand he holdeth a golden crozier and in his right hand he useth a pair of goldsmiths' tongs. Beneath these steps of ascension to his chair, in opposition to St. Dunstan, is properly painted a goldsmiths' forge and furnace, with fire and gold in it, a workman blowing with his bellows. On his right and left hand there is a large press of gold and silver plate, representing a shop of trade; and further, in front, are several artificers at work on anvils with hammers, beating out plate fit for the forging and formation of several vessels of gold and silver."

Also represented were an assay master, finers, wiredrawers and miners, and

"The Devil also appearing to St. Dunstan, is catched by the nose at a proper qu, which is given in his speech. When the speech is spoken, the great anvil is set forth, with a silversmith holding on it a plate of massive silver, and three other workmen at work, keeping excellent time in their strokes upon the anvil."

St. Eloi, the regular patron saint of smiths, indeed of all workers in metal—also known as St. Lo or St. Eligius—had an anvil for his emblem, and seems to have been a metal worker himself. Born of poor parents near Limoges, in the seventh century, he was apprenticed to a goldsmith at Limoges. Always the goldsmiths seem to steal the picture! St. Eloi, King Dagobert's Master of the Mint, and Bishop of Noyon, utilized his art in the making of sacred vessels for the church and beautiful shrines for saints. The importance of the smith at this period is suggested in an old French song of many verses, in which St. Eloi is described as speaking in decidedly familiar fashion to his king. One of these verses runs:

Le Roi Dagobert
Mettait ses culottes à l'envers.
Le bon St. Eloi

Lui disait, "Oh, mon roi,
Votre majesté est mal culotté."
"C'est vrai," lui dit le roi,
"Mon pere ye etait avant moi."

Other verses are unprintable!

Like St. Dunstan, St. Eloi was alleged to have been
tormented by the Demon while at his work, and, like St
Dunstan too, St. Eloi seized him by the nose with the red-hot
pincers. St. Eloi being earlier than St. Dunstan, one would
have thought that one experience of the kind would have been
sufficient for the archfiend. On another occasion, a horse which
was brought to be shod was possessed of the devil and kicked
so furiously that no one dared to touch it. The saint cut off his
leg, put on the shoe, and then, with the sign of the Cross,
joined the leg on, to the astonishment of all. Another, apparently
earlier, version of the story relates that the king bade St. Loy
to shoe his horses with silver shoes—not inappropriately,
seeing that St. Eloi was more a smith in precious metals than
a blacksmith—and the saint, having cut off the four limbs,
shod them and replaced them without harm to the animal.
A youth tried to imitate him, but only succeeded in killing the
horse, which the saint then restored to life, after gently chiding
the youth for his presumption.

Baring-Gould, in his *Lives of the Saints*, states that St. Eloi
or Eligius was

> "in art represented erroneously as a farrier, with a horse's
> leg in his hand, on account of the story, and numerous works
> of art of the fifteenth or sixteenth century are recorded as
> figuring him either as standing with a horse's foot in his
> hand, after having cut it off to fit it with the shoe, or, on
> the basis of the other legend, as gripping with his tongs the
> nose of a devil disguised as a woman".

The legendary miracle of the shoeing crops up again and again
in smith stories, and one might almost be made to believe that
the practice was a common one among divine or saintly smiths
of the Christian era!

Arthur Mee, in the "King's England" series, writes that
"when workmen were repairing the church" of Freckenham,

Suffolk, in 1776, there came to light a small alabaster panel,
of quite uncertain age, but probably of the fourteenth century.
It depicted a blacksmith holding a horse's leg on an anvil
with one hand and a hammer in the other. "Close by is a horse
standing on three legs, with a bonneted groom, or maybe its
master, holding it. The smith is thought to be St. Eloy. . . ."
In the porch of the church at Wincanton, Somerset, there is
a sculptured panel showing St. Eloi, dressed as a bishop,
standing with one leg of a horse in his arms, before a forge,
while the horse waits on three legs on the other side. Yet another
such sculpture of St. Eloi or St. Leger is to be seen over the
south door of Durweston church, in Dorset.

At the chapel of St. Eloi, near Landerneau, in Brittany,
there is also a representation of St. Eloi holding the fetlock of
a horse in one hand, the hoof resting on an anvil, whilst with
the other hand the saint hammers at the shoe on the hoof;
beside him stands the horse, minus his off forefoot. Here, a
remarkable custom is observed at a Pardon held at the chapel.
All the farmers from the district around bring their horses,
and every horse is made to bow its head as it passes in procession
the statue of the saint, on whose altar a wisp of hair, from
either the tail or the mane of the horse, is placed. Pardons of
St. Eloi are also held at St. Nicholas de Plelem, where, too, an
offering is made from the mane, and near Sizon.

St. Eloi was no mere legendary smith. He founded two
distinct corporations of goldsmiths, one for secular and one for
religious works. After a disastrous fire in the goldsmiths' quarter
of Paris, they established a colony under the patronage of St.
Eloi in the shadow of the church of St. Paul des Champs,
subsequently removing to the Grand-Pont; goldsmiths were
rather fond of trading on bridges. Eloi had also established, in
631, a goldsmiths' school in the Abbey of Solignac, at Limoges.
The first abbot, Thillon, was a pupil of the saint and a skilful
goldsmith; the monastery preserved, through several centuries,
the traditions of its founder, and furnished models and skilled
workmen to the monastic ateliers exclusively manufacturing
plate for the churches. Under the administration of its first
Abbess, St. Anne, the monastery of S. Martial, too, became a
branch of the goldsmiths' school.[1]

[1] *The Arts in the Middle Ages* (Paul Lacroix).

St. Clement seems to have been pre-eminently the patron saint of blacksmiths, though his only connection with the smithy seems to have been that he was martyred by being thrown in the sea tied to an anchor—just as St. Adrian is shown with an anvil because his limbs were struck off on one, before he was beheaded. When wondering why he should ever have been chosen as the patron saint of smiths, though, one must remember that he belongs to a far earlier period—the first century—than either St. Eloi or St. Dunstan, and therefore had a start, at a time when no doubt blacksmiths, or other smiths proper, were not renowned for their piety. His emblem is an anchor, and the story of his martyrdom appears to belong to the fourth century A.D.

Because of his association with the anchor, there seems some relevancy in the fact that "Old Clem" was personated in a procession of the blacksmiths of Chatham Dockyard early in the nineteenth century. Under the same nickname, he was also personated in Sussex, home of a dead and gone iron-working industry. His day, December 4th, was observed, too, in the north of England. In recent years, however, the most elaborate honours paid to him were perpetuated in a Hampshire village, Twyford, where the "Clem Supper" was held at the Bugle Inn, on St. Clement's Day, up to about 1880. The toast of the evening was "The Blacksmiths" and this was followed by the reading of the blacksmiths' legend of King Solomon:

"It came to pass when Solomon, the Son of David, had finished the Temple of Jerusalem, that he called unto him the chief architects, the head architects, the head artificers, and cunning workers in silver and gold, in wood and ivory, and in stone, yea, all who had aided in rearing the Temple of the Lord, and he said unto them, 'Sit ye down at my table. I have prepared a feast for all the cunning artificers and chief workers. Stretch forth your hands, therefore, and eat and drink and be merry. Is not the labourer worthy of his hire? Is not the skilful artificer worthy of his honour? Muzzle not the ox that treadeth out the corn.' And when Solomon and the chief workers were seated, and the fatness of the land and the wine and oil thereof were set upon the table, there came one who knocked loudly at the door and thrust himself into the festal chamber. Then Solomon the King was wroth and the stranger said, 'When men wish to honour me they call me the Son of the Forge, but when they desire to mock me they call me the blacksmith: and seeing that the toil of working in the fire covers me with sweat and smut, the latter name, O King, is not inapt, and in that thy servant desires no better.' 'But,' said Solomon, 'why come ye thus rudely and unbidden to the feast where none but the chief workers of the Temple are invited?' 'Please you, my Lord, I came rudely,' replied the man, 'because thy servants obliged me to force my way, but I came not unbidden. Was it not proclaimed that the chief workmen of the Temple are invited with the King of Israel?' Then he who carved the cherubim said, 'This fellow is no sculptor.' And he who inlaid the roof with pure gold said, 'Neither is he a worker in fine metals.' And he who raised the walls said, 'He is no cutter in stone.' And he who made the roof cried out, 'He is not cunning in cedar wood, neither knoweth he the mystery of knitting strange pieces of timber together.' Then said Solomon, 'What has thou to say, Son of the Forge, why I should not order thee to be plucked by the beard, scourged by the scourge, and stoned to death with stones?' And when the Son of the Forge heard this, he was in no sort dismayed, but advancing to the table snatched up and swallowed a cup of wine and said, 'O King, live for ever. The chief workers in wood and gold and stone have said I am not of them and they have said truly. I am their superior. Before they lived I was created. I am their master and they are my servants!' And he turned him round and said to the chief carver in stone, 'Who made the tools with which you carve?' And he said, 'The blacksmith.' And he said to the chief mason, 'Who made the chisel with which the stones of the temple were squared?' And he said, 'The blacksmith.' And he said to the chief worker in wood, 'Who made the tools with which you felled the trees of Lebanon and made into the pillars and roof of the temple?' And he answered, 'The blacksmith.' 'Enough, enough, good fellow,' said Solomon, 'thou hast proved that I invited thee and thou art all men's father. Go and wash the smut of the forge from thy face and come and sit at my right hand. The chief

of workmen are but men, thou art more.' So it happene
that the feast of Solomon and the blacksmiths has bee:
honoured ever since."[1]

The dating and origin of this tradition are obscure, but i
traditional ceremony connected with Solomon's Temple th
place of Tubal-Cain, the artificer, is one of honour. Since
however, there was no hammer heard in the Temple while i
was building, the whole story emphasizes the unwarrante(
obscurity which so often is the lot of the worker behind th
scenes. There is also an echo of the superiority assumed by th
workers of precious metals, as compared with the worker i
iron, despite the fact, constantly emerging in ancient history
that the ironworker was originally a worker in all other metal
as well.

There is, however, as with so many folk-tales, anothe
version of the story, very different in setting, though pointin{
the same moral. A king[2] wished to build himself a palace, s(
called together all the master craftsmen for the purpose, an(
announced that the man doing the best work would be calle(
"Father of All Craftsmen". When the castle was finished, th
king was so pleased with the way in which they had laboure(
that he gave a big banquet and commanded all the craftsmei
to attend, in their traditional clothes and bearing their tools
at this feast the "Father of All Craftsmen" would be chosei
and set at the head of the table. The choice was difficult
mason, sculptor, smith, all had done their work to perfection
Eventually, he got out of the difficulty by appointing his tailor
who, though he had had nothing to do with the building o:
the palace, was essential to the robing of the king himself ir
gracing the structure.

At the end of the banquet, all the guests went home excep
the blacksmith, who disappeared into the forest. Then, whei
the mason wanted new tools, there was no one to make them
no one to make chisels for the carpenter, no one to mend th(
broken hinges of the palace gates, no one to shoe the king'
horses. The tailor's scissors broke and could not be repaired
Even the warriors could not fight without a smith. So the kin{

[1] Proceedings of the Hampshire Field Club.
[2] One version says King Alfred.

ommanded search to be made for the smith, who was found in
cave.[1] Then the king called another feast and announced that,
ince none of the others could work without the smith, he must
e "Father of All Craftsmen" and sit at the head of the table.

All agreed, except the tailor, who, angry at his displacement,
rept under the festive board and snipped pieces out of the
lacksmith's apron with his scissors. That, it is said, is why
miths cut a fringe on the bottoms of their leather aprons. Still
nother version of the story, however, was told the author by
fr. Elmes, of Wareham, Dorset, representative of a long line
f rural smiths. In this, the banquet was given by the squire,
vho omitted to invite the blacksmith until the latter threatened
o shoe his horses no more. Then, on his way to the banquet,
he smith went to the kitchen, where he became so engaged in
lalliance with one of the maids as not to notice the jealous, or
nischievous, tailor snipping his apron.

In the Twyford ritual, the final episode was "firing the
nvil". A little hole in the anvil was filled with gunpowder,
:overed by a plug, through which a hole was bored, and the
harge was set off by a train: or, fireworks were exploded on
he anvil. Sometimes there was a procession, with an effigy of
it. Clement, to raise funds for the feast in the evening, the
ffigy finishing up outside the inn, with the blacksmiths inside.

It is a little difficult to be sure whether the ceremony of
'firing the anvil" originated with the St. Clement celebrations
ir was only incorporated into them. Mr. Norman Wymer, in
Country Crafts, dates the practice, which obtains in Sussex,
Iampshire and possibly Kent, back to the Armada period,
vhen a plan was arranged whereby blacksmiths in certain areas
vhere communications were bad were to pass on invasion
varnings to outlying villages by igniting gunpowder on their
nvils. When the invasion failed to materialize, the smiths
lecided to celebrate Drake's victory in this way instead, and
he practice of signalling the end of war on the anvil grew. Mr.
Nymer cites the case of a blacksmith who fired his anvil at
he conclusion of the Boer War, and suggests that the end of
he 1914–18 war was notified to some villagers in the same way.[2]

---

[1] In one account, he returns leaning on the arm of St. Clement.
[2] Several smiths today can testify to the practice, without, however,
ssociating it with St. Clement or the Armada.

St. Clement, anyway, had nothing to do with gunpowder, and it looks rather as if the Armada provision had struck the Twyford blacksmiths as being a good idea for making a noise—always, it would appear, a necessary part of a celebration.

Hone's Everyday Book, the author's copy of which is dated 1826, gives an account of an annual ceremony, on the evening of St. Clement's Day, by the blacksmiths' apprentices of Woolwich Dockyard. One of the senior apprentices, being chosen to serve as "Old Clem", was attired in a great coat, having his head covered with an oakham wig, his face masked, and a long white beard; so attired, he sat in a large wooden chair, with a crown and anchor made of wood on the top, and, around it, four transparencies, representing "the blacksmiths' arms", "anchor smiths at work", "Britannia with her anchor" and "Mount Etna", a curious mixture of the current epoch with classical times reminiscent of the Cornish and other folk plays. Old Clem had before him a wooden anvil, and in his hands a pair of tongs and a wooden hammer, with which he punctuated his speech. A mate, also masked, attended him with a wooden sledge-hammer and other attendants surrounded him, some carrying torches, banners, flags, etc. The procession, headed by a drum and fife, and six men with old Clem mounted on their shoulders, proceeded around the town, stopping for refreshments at each of the fairly numerous public houses, and calling on the blacksmiths and officers of the dockyard with money-boxes. At each call, after the mate had called for order with

"Gentlemen all, attention give,
And wish St. Clem, long, long to live"

Old Clem himself made the following speech:

"I am the real St. Clement, the first founder of brass, iron, and steel, from the ore. I have been to Mount Etna, where the god Vulcan first built his forge, and forged the armour and thunderbolts for the god Jupiter. I have been through the deserts of Arabia; through Asia, Africa, and America; through the city of Pongrove; through the town of Tipmingo; and all the northern parts of Scotland. I arrived in London on the twenty-third of November, and came down to his majesty's dockyard at Woolwich, to see how all the gentlemen Vulcans came on there. I found them all hard at work, and wish to leave them well on the twenty-fourth."

lmost a complete traditional history!
The mate then added:

"Come all you Vulcans stout and strong,
Unto St. Clem we do belong,
I know this house is well prepared
With plenty of money and good strong beer,
And we must drink before we part,
All for to cheer each merry heart,
Come all you Vulcans, strong and stout,
Unto St. Clem I pray turn out;
For now St. Clem's going round the town,
His coach and six goes merrily round,
Huzza-a-a."

On completion of the round and the collection, they djourned to a public house for a supper on the proceeds, bviously already "well oiled".

St. Martin comes into association with the smiths by virtue f being the patron saint of all who travel on horseback, and aving a horseshoe as his emblem. A traveller of the Middle ges would often, when having his horse shod for a long and langerous journey, have an extra shoe made to hang inside the loor or porch of a chapel or church to ensure the protection of t. Martin. This, it is suggested, was the origin of hanging torseshoes on doors for luck. The ordinary person hangs his torseshoe points upwards, "to keep the luck in"; blacksmiths lang them points down, "to pour the luck out on the forge". he three horseshoes in the Farriers' Company's arms, and the ne in those of the Royal Veterinary College, are shown with oints downwards.

CHAPTER X

THE MEDIAEVAL SMITH

And he sang, "Hurrah for my handiwork!"
And the red sparks lit the air;
Not alone for the blade was the bright steel made,
And he fashioned the first plough-share.

CHARLES MACKAY: *Tubal-Cain.*

IT IS a curious thing that, despite the cult of the smith amon
Teutonic races, there is little on record with regard to smithcra:
in Anglo-Saxon times in England. Much of the activities of th
forge must still have been devoted to the production of weapon:
but the Saxons were agriculturalists as well as warriors, an
the work of the smith must have been evident in the fields an
farms. It is also self-evident on church doors, in hinges an
scrollwork, and in some cases in defensive plating and met:
rims, peculiar to England and Scandinavia.

By the time of the Norman Conquest of England, smithie
had been established as rural necessities, and in them plough
shares and other implements were forged and oxen shod fo
work in the fields. Sixty-four smiths are recorded in th
Domesday Survey, six of them in Hereford having each t
make for the king a hundred and twenty horseshoes yearly
The smiths ranked as manorial officers; on the Continen
under Charlemagne, too, they were skilled tradesmen, rankin
above the ordinary serf.

Already, at the Domesday period, Gloucestershire, mor
especially the Forest of Dean, was a source of the productio:
of iron articles, apart from the ubiquitous local smithing, and
in the reign of Henry II, there was a constant output of iro:
bars, nails, pickaxes and hammers for the king's—and other—
building operations, horseshoes for the army, arrows and othe
war products.[1]

The craft of the blacksmith, according to some historian:

---

[1] *English Industries of the Middle Ages* (Salzman). The Rockingham Fore:
area of Northants was also a centre of iron production from the twelfth to th
fifteenth century.

reached its zenith in the thirteenth
century. The period extending
from the Early Iron Age to the
fourteenth century is often referred to as being specifically the
"Smith's Age", and is described
by J. Starkie Gardner (in *Ironwork*,
1927) as the period of "genuine
blacksmithing". The early craftsmen relied almost entirely upon
anvil, hammer, bellows and fire,

Twelfth-century smithwork

vice and chisel; they trusted their eye for measurement and
for design.[1] Yet they produced such work as the grille around
Queen Eleanor's tomb in Westminster Abbey, made by Master
Thomas Leighton, of Leighton Buzzard, Bedfordshire.

During the thirteenth century the Wealden iron industry
in Sussex challenged the pre-eminence of the Forest of Dean in
the south of England; in 1254, the Sheriff of Sussex was called
upon to provide 30,000 horseshoes and 60,000 nails, and in 1275
Master Henry of Lewes, the king's smith, purchased 406 iron
rods in the Weald for £16 17s. 11d., similar transactions
following.[2]

In the north of England a good deal of forging, as well as
smelting, was in the hands of the monasteries, and especially
the Cistercian houses, always to the fore in agriculture, the
principal rival of war in the utilization of the blacksmiths'
products, and their principal market once the trade of the
armourer became a separate speciality. At the end of the
thirteenth century, the forges belonging to the Cistercians of
Furness Abbey, probably at least forty in number, yielded a
profit of £6 13s. 4d. in a year, as against the profit on flocks
and herds of only £3 11s. 3d. Both smelting-houses and forges
were often itinerant, as in earlier days, and when Fountains
Abbey, another Cistercian foundation, was given forges in
Nidderdale, the monks were expressly given the right to move
them from one place to another.[3]

Apart from such operations, where the whole process, from

---

[1] Dr. Iorwerth Peate, in the "Guide to the Collection illustrating Welsh Folk
Craft, etc.," National Museum of Wales.
[2] *English Industries of the Middle Ages* (Salzman).   [3] Ibid.

F

digging ore onwards, was carried on, many of the other monasteries had their own smiths forging ironwork for them, making hinges, the massive locks and keys for the doors, and the railings which hemmed in the sacred part about the altar. Often, too, the monastic smith made the great corona or candelabrum. As a German historian[1] has written:

> "With the thirteenth century appears to have come in that kind of door which, by the artistic style of its mountings, gives a splendid testimony to the workmanship of the blacksmith of the time. These mountings are spread out over the surface in symmetrical branches, ending in conventional foliage, happily filling up the space as the ivy spreads its branches over walls."

In Scandinavia, too, in the twelfth and thirteenth centuries, smiths were forging exquisite and highly decorative products, including the ironwork of church doors, using Roman and native traditional designs, interlacing, ringwork, dragons, etc. —paganism intruding itself upon Christian workmanship.

Mr. Martin Briggs,[2] dealing with the architectural aspect, speaks of a new wave of influence passing over English art in the thirteenth century, and "nowhere is its effect more apparent than in the smith's craft". This he ascribes to the influence of intercourse with the East, but, he adds, "even before the end of the fourteenth century the English smith had lost his position of pre-eminence to the Continental metalworker". On the other hand, the art of the Scandinavian smith, too, had declined in the fourteenth century.

During the later Middle Ages, the smith figures prominently as a necessary companion to the masons, in accounts of the building of great structures, especially where quarrying was involved and the consequent wear and tears of tools is great. At Carnarvon Castle, where quarrying took place, there were five smiths employed, to thirty-two hewers, twenty-five layers and thirty-four quarriers, as against two smiths at most to seventy hewers—with no quarrying at the site—at Eton

---

[1] *Ecclesiastical Art in Germany During the Middle Ages* (Dr. Wilhelm Lubke).
[2] *A Short History of the Building Crafts.*

College, in the fifteenth century. At Beaumaris Castle, in the winter of 1316–17, one smith and one assistant were employed in making "gadds" or pieces of iron and in sharpening the instruments of the ten cementarii (hewers), six cubitores (layers) and nine quarriers, the smith being paid twopence for each iron and a halfpenny for sharpening each gadd. The money paid to smiths at York Minster, for "repairing of masons' tools", ranged from 77s. in 1371 to 81s. or 82s. in the early years of the fifteenth century. At Kirby Mixtoe Castle, in 1481, a smith was paid twopence per dozen for sharpening the masons' axes and chisels. At the Tudor castle of Sandgate (1539–40), the smith was paid ten shillings per hundred for sharpening the masons' irons or points, twopence each for battering of hammers, twopence each for battering axes, and threepence each for steeling masons' axes, and their irons or points.[1]

It is, however, with the ordinary individual smith of the countryside that we are more concerned. The town craftsmen, here and on the Continent, belonged to highly organized guilds; the rural smiths were individual workers, making simple objects for everyday use. In the thirteenth century, nearly every village or manor had at least one smith attending to agricultural needs, shoeing horses or oxen on annual contracts, and making useful articles for farm and home at low prices— a hammer for a penny or a billhook for sixpence.[2]

The village smith was a man of less substance than the miller, but essential to the needs of other crafts and an expert on rural necessities. The duty of finding a smith devolved on a particular holding; the village smith's widow at Aldingbourne, Sussex, is recorded as owing duties of shoeing for the lord, and mending his ploughs—the latter for nothing. She had twenty-five pence for fifty horseshoes with eight holes and fifty with six holes, for the lord, one penny for the four shoes of the steward's horse whenever he came, also those of the sergeant and the carter.[3] There is no evidence that she actually did the work, though Ronald Sett[4] speaks of an Esthonian smith who

[1] The Mediaeval Mason (Knoop and Jones).
[2] English Country Crafts (Norman Wymer).
[3] English Villagers of the Thirteenth Century (Homer).
[4] Baltic Corner, 1937.

was assisted by his wife at busy times—and women forged nails, in the Midlands, in the eighteenth century. The English mediaeval smith of the manor got his charcoal from the lord's wood, dined in hall when the lord was in residence, and had his land ploughed by the lord's ploughs, since he was a land-holder as well as a smith.[1] He made all the farm implements, with materials supplied by the bailiff, and undertook the shoeing of the horses of the community for a year, supplying his own material.[2]

At Oakham, Rutlandshire, the horseshoe appears as a toll payable to the castle, every peer of the realm passing through the town having still to contribute one, which is now hung in the castle hall; the custom is said to have originated with noble-men who refused to pay toll having to forfeit a shoe from one of their horses.

Small tenants, exempt from boon work for the manor, holding insufficient land to support them,[3] and not sharing in the common fields, grew in numbers and importance during the Middle Ages:[4] they were smiths, carpenters, and other crafts-men, identifiable by their names or nicknames, Smith, Faber, Ironmonger, le Ferrour, among the metal workers.[5] Benet Smith (faber) on the Bishop of Chichester's manor of Amberley, in Sussex, held only four acres belonging to the smithy, and in return for this he had to mend, with the lord's iron,[6] all the iron gear belonging to two ploughs, but doing nothing new; he had to shoe two horses and the sergeant's horses with the lord's

---

[1] *English Villagers of the Thirteenth Century* (Homer).

[2] *Life and Work of the People of England* (Dorothy Hartley and Margaret Elliott).

[3] According to Professor Henri Frankfurt (*The Birth of Civilisation in the Near East*), every citizen in Mesopotamia, "whether priest, merchant or craftsman", was also a practical farmer who worked his allotment to support himself and his dependants, and smiths, who, among others, received allow-ances in a Sumerian temple city, also held allotments on the temple lands. Mr. Gordon Childe, however, suggests that the smith's allotment may have been cultivated for him, so that he could devote his time to his craft.

[4] At Crawley, Hants, 1448–49, John, son of Stephen, a villein, paid 8*d.* per annum to use the craft of smith with John Starlynge, and to stay with him as an apprentice. *Economic and Social History of an English Village* (N. S. B. Gras).

[5] Smith, from "smite", is Anglo-Saxon—though this derivation has been disputed. Farrier, from "ferrier", ironworker, is Norman.

[6] Professor Thorold Rogers states that, in the thirteenth century, iron was purchased and stocked by the bailiff and debited to the smith as served out to him.

iron, and receive nothing, also to grind all the scythes used in the lord's meadows and all the shears while they sheared the lord's sheep.

Mediaeval accounts, though, also show payments made to the smith and carpenter for repairing and making ploughs, carts, agricultural implements, etc.

An illustration of a thirteenth-century smith at work shows him with a leather apron, and, like Vulcan, with his head covered. The blacksmith's shop was usually open on all sides but roofed over, and, as throughout the ages, was a favourite resort for gathering and disseminating village news.

The smiths of the towns were somewhat differently placed and quickly divided into specialist trades.[1] That they were family craftsmen still in the earlier Middle Ages—as indeed they have remained to a large degree since—is suggested by their names. At a Coroner's Inquest at Oxford in 1297, the jurymen include Geoffrey le Smith, of the parish of St. Aldate's; another, in 1301, is John le Smith, from the parish of All Saints.[2] Even in the sixteenth century, Nicholas Smith and Richard Smith are smiths in Poole, and a number of Smiths appear as town councillors in the Taunton records for the fifteenth to seventeenth centuries who may well have been smiths by trade.

In Colchester, early in the fourteenth century, with about three thousand inhabitants and three hundred and fifty-nine houses, there were twenty-nine trades, including that of the blacksmith. Of ten smiths there in 1300, the stocks in trade of six, including hammers, anvils, and other implements, and iron, were only valued at eighteen pence., 3s., 5s., 7s., 10s. and 20s. respectively. J. de Columb, the wealthiest smith in the town, had his property valued at £3, but his implements only accounted for 8s. and his stock of iron 2s. The whole town, though, was only valued, for the purpose of taxation, at £518.

Smiths were a hardworking fraternity. The blacksmiths of London worked, at the end of the fourteenth century, from dawn until 9 p.m., except during November, December and January, when they worked from 6 a.m. to 8 p.m., but, against

[1] The Ironmongers' Company of London, in the fourteenth century, were merchants and traders, with warehouses and shops, purchasing manufactured articles from working smiths in town and country.
[2] *Life in the Middle Ages* (Coulton).

these long hours, there were frequent holidays, Sundays, greater festivals, local festivals, and on Saturdays and the eves of the festivals work ceased, as a rule, at four o'clock, or earlier. Night work was frowned upon by the authorities, partly because of bad workmanship, but partly because of the nuisance to others: the blacksmiths were particularly regarded as causing nuisance. The worst of the complaints, however, were lodged against one of the offshoots of smithing, for many of the spurriers were alleged to be

"wandering about all day without working at all at their trade, and then, when they have become drunk and frantic, they take to their work, to the annoyance of the sick and all their neighbourhood . . . and then they blow up their fires so vigorously that their forges begin all at once to blaze, to the great peril of themselves and of all the neighbourhood round".[1]

An earlier and more technical complaint, that certain unskilled ferrores, or farriers, who had set up forges in London city, had caused the loss of many horses, led to the formation of the Farriers' Company in 1356.

By the fourteenth century, English wrought ironwork was very good, despite the great artistry of the Continental smiths calling forth Briggs' comparison, and hardware almost everywhere was of excellent quality, mostly made by local smiths. Prices are recorded of three farthings for a hammer, 6d. for another, obviously larger, billhooks at 6d. and 1s., a cauldron, one of the earliest peaceful products of the smith, 11s. 8d.; lath nails for timber and slate buildings were sold by local smiths at the rate of 10,000, or one bag, for 10s.[2] Virtually all the utensils of the home, at this time, were being made either on the establishments themselves, where large enough, or by local tradesmen, smiths, ironworkers, potters, woodworkers; often the mediaeval kitchen was the craftsman's workship. The smith was an ingenious fellow, too. In 1481, the Tuckers' Guild at Bristol paid 8s. 1½d. to "the smyth", in connection with a piece of

[1] Salzman, quoting Riley, "Mems of London", in *English Industries of the Middle Ages*.
[2] *Life and Work of the English People* (Hartley and Elliott).

mechanism—an "image"—for turning the spit, a task that should not have been very difficult for a craft which so often made the church clocks, then, and long after.

Craftsman, artist, inventor, man of resource—often enough the smith was warrior, too. A Cornish rising of 1496 was headed by Thomas Flamode, a lawyer, and Michael Joseph, a blacksmith, of Bodmin, both, says Stow, "men of stout stomachs". They reached Blackheath, before being defeated, and the heads of lawyer and blacksmith subsequently adorned London Bridge.

The "Valiant Blacksmith" of Aachen, in the Middle Ages, who defeated with his bare hands the Count of Juelich, when he tried to take the city, was more fortunate. A statue to his memory now stands in his native city, to commemorate the "sturdy independence of the burgher who trounced the insolent nobleman", and a pseudo-Order of the Valiant Blacksmith is bestowed, at carnival time, on popular citizens.

Sir Walter Scott's description of Henry Gow, in *The Fair Maid of Perth*, is probably typical of the burgher-smith. He was

"rather below the middle stature, but the breadth of his shoulders, the length and brawniness of his arms, and the muscular appearance of the whole man argued an unusual share of strength and a frame kept in vigour by constant exercise. His legs were somewhat bent, but not in a manner which could be said to approach to deformity; on the contrary, which seemed to correspond to the strength of his frame, though it injured in some degree its symmetry. His dress was of buff-hide, and he wore, in a belt around his waist, a heavy broadside and a dirk or poniard, as to defend his purse, which, burgher fashion, was attached to the same cincture."

The turbulent area in which the scene is set, of course, argues for so much armament, and Gow apparently travelled to sell his wares. He is drawn as an armourer, though the armourer's trade at this time, the close of the fourteenth century, was largely separated from that of the ordinary smith. Catherine, the Fair Maid, draws the distinction between the two great phases of the smith's craft:

"If you renounce the forging of swords and bucklers, there remains to you the task of forming the harmless spade and the honourable as well as useful ploughshare—of those implements which contribute to the support of life or to its comfort. Thou canst frame locks and bars to defend the property of the weak against the stouthrief and oppressing of the strong. . . ."[1]

In that, we see the Middle Ages standing at the parting of the ways, in the past the smith serving both warrior and farmer, in the future the trades of armourer and blacksmith distinct, though the locksmith is still not envisaged as the specialist he was to become. Still, though, Caxton's smith of the chessboard stood for "all maner of werkemen", carrying in his left hand a square to represent carpentry, in his girdle a trowel for masonry, and in his right hand a hammer to symbolize all kinds of smiths, "And to alle these crafty men but apperteyneth that they be trewe, wise and stronge, and hit is here that they have in hemself truth and loyaltie."

At the close of the Middle Ages, the ironworkers were still "smiths", but specializing more and more. Of Birmingham, Leland wrote, in 1538:

"There be many smiths in the town, that used to make knives and all manner of cutting tools, and many loriners that make bits, and a great many naylors, so that a great part of the town is maintained by smiths, who have their iron and sea-coal out of Staffordshire."

---

[1] As a practical demonstration of Catherine's sentiments, during the United States presidential campaign of 1952, "Bishop" Bass, of "the Church of God Bible Party", staged a week-long peace conference in Alabama, and, after taking a course of lessons from a blacksmith, beat a dozen swords into ploughshares before a cheering crowd!

CHAPTER XI

THE SMITH GUILDS

IN ANCIENT days, when crafts were few in number and comprehensive in their scope, that of the smith, be he iron-worker or a worker in all kinds of metals, was one of those almost invariably present. In urban communities, like crafts-men tended to band themselves together, in quarters, in craft guilds, or both. There are even smith guilds in primitive African society, with initiation ceremonies and secret cults. In ancient Rome, guilds of artisans were formed at an early stage—in the days of King Numa, it is said—and the nine listed as funda-mental include, in addition to the archaic craft of the potter, smiths and goldsmiths.[1]

Having regard to the importance and universality of the smiths' craft in the Middle Ages and the early tendency to form guilds, one would expect perhaps to find a guild of smiths in all the major mediaeval towns of Europe. Actually, the smiths' guilds were not numerous. There are two likely reasons for this. In the first place, a good deal of smiths' work was done in the villages, on the manor estates, and where there were smiths in the towns they were often too few in number to form a separate guild. Secondly, while the prehistoric and legendary smith was a metal worker in general, and later smiths were concerned with all kinds of ironwork, the growing importance and variety of metal working led to the division and subdivision of the originai craft. In the Middle Ages, goldsmiths and copper-smiths, as well as blacksmiths, and the iron founder, the iron-monger and the armourer were specialists in their own trades, as well as the spurriers, the cutlers, and other workers in ferrous metals.

The fact that such crafts were really refinements of smiths' work, or that the trades marketed smiths' products, should

---

[1] There was a college of smiths at Bath who attended to the burial of one Julius Vitalis, a smith of the Twentieth Legion, stationed at Chester, a Belgian with nine years' service, who died at the age of twenty-nine. In early Roman days, when soldiers were graded and armed according to social status, smiths, for field repair work, were attached to the more heavily armed classes.

naturally suggest a combination in a common guild. Actually, this did happen in a few cases, but not many, and sometimes a composite guild included crafts having no common ancestry. That the Smiths' Guilds at Preston and Shrewsbury included armourers is a perfectly logical thing. That, in the sixteenth century, the Smiths' Guild at Boston, Lincolnshire, covered smiths, farriers, braziers and cutlers is consistent with the original position of metal workers. But the Smiths' Guild at Gloucester included, not only ironmongers and cutlers, but saddlers and glaziers as well. At Norwich, the smaller crafts were grouped into composite guilds, including one of various kinds of smiths: in 1449, the bladesmiths, locksmiths and loriners were constrained to link up with the Smiths' Guild. At Ludlow, in 1575, the Fellowship and Brotherhood of Smiths—commonly called the Hammermen's Company—included fletchers (arrowmakers), bowyers, goldsmiths, ironmongers, cardmakers, saddlers, coopers, cutlers, pewterers, braziers, nailers, armourers, makers of sieves or tugars, and hawkers of bend.[1] An amalgamation in post-mediaeval times brought the smiths, cutlers, pewterers, plumbers, founders, cardmakers, girdlers, wiredrawers, spurriers, arrowheadmakers, armourers and bellfounders into one Company at Chester.

In France, the goldsmiths were separated from their auxiliary trades in the time of Louis IX, and given a privileged position of exemption from the service of the Watch. In the provinces, however, they were often united with other trades. At Guise they were linked with farriers, coppersmiths and locksmiths, and bore on their banner a horseshoe, a mallet and a key. Elsewhere, they were united with pewterers, slaters, and even grocers.[2]

In Chesterfield, there was a guild of smiths from early times, but their numbers were few, and in 1387 they were amalgamated with the Guild of Holy Cross of Merchants. The incorporation of a body of men whose members were too few to form a distinctive craft or trade guild into a religious guild was not an out-of-the-way procedure. It seems, though, a little strange that the absorption should have been into a Merchants' Guild —the Merchants' Guilds usually considering themselves in a

[1] *The Mediaeval Mason* (Knoop and Jones).
[2] *Arts in the Middle Ages* (Lacroix).

superior class to those of the crafts, so much so that the struggle
for power between the Merchant or Trade Companies and the
Craft Companies of London is guild history.

In London, there was a blacksmiths' fraternity of St. Eloy
in the fourteenth century, and when the original thirty-two
mysteries or trades were increased in 1376, they then included
the Blacksmiths (1372),[1] the Spurriers (1344), the Farriers (1356),
Armourers, Goldsmiths, Cutlers and Ironmongers: the Founders

were incorporated in 1389. In the
sixteenth century, the Blacksmiths absorbed the Spurriers,
the Armourers, the Bladesmiths
and the Braziers, and the Girdlers, the Pinners and Wiresellers.
The Livery Companies of the
City of London today include
Goldsmiths, Ironmongers,
Cutlers, Armourers, Founders,
Blacksmiths, Farriers and
Loriners, in that order of pre-
cedence, but only the first two
rank as "great" companies.

Arms of the Worshipful Company of Farriers

Goldsmiths Companies, though not numerous in the mediaeval
cities, were usually prominent and powerful, by reason of their
wealth, and the goldsmiths themselves tended to congregate in
lucrative areas, London Bridge and the Rialto Bridge at Venice
being favoured localities, though Foster Lane, in London city,
was a goldsmiths' quarter.

In the procession of London crafts to meet Richard II's
bride, Anne of Bohemia, all the mysteries of the city wore red
and black liveries. The Goldsmiths had, on the red of their
dresses, bars of silver work and silver trefoils, and each of the
seven score goldsmiths wore, on the black part, five knots of
gold and silk, and on their worshipful heads red hats powdered
with silver trefoils. In Edward IV's reign, the Goldsmiths'
liverymen wore violet and scarlet; under Henry VII, violet
gowns and black hoods, reverting to violet and scarlet in the
reign of his successor.

[1] There was a London Company of Blacksmiths in the thirteenth century
who were also the toothdrawers!

The Blacksmiths' sphere of influence in London was prescribed as a four-mile circuit, in addition to the city and suburbs—which was about the average given to the metropolitan guilds. Apart from the liverymen, a brotherhood of "yeomen", or journeymen, was admitted to a subordinate share in the Blacksmiths' fraternity in 1434, but by the late sixteenth and seventeenth centuries the term "yeoman" was being applied to masters and traders as well.

Bristol and Hereford had Cutlers' Guilds, separately from the Smiths. There were Smiths' Guilds at Winchester, Coventry, Chester, Canterbury, York, Newcastle-on-Tyne, and Bodmin—the last dedicated to Saints Dunstan and Eloy.

At Canterbury, the Smiths and Armourers kept their feast on "St. Loy's day". There, the business of the smiths was laid down as "shoeing" wheels as well as horses, making bars, spring locks, catches and latches, nails, and "squaring" spindles for water mills and horse mills. They might work no French iron, save for bars to be set in timber, nor stock locks except for seasoned wood. At the close of the Middle Ages, their charges were laid down as 2*d*. for a stock-lock key, 3*d*. for a hollow door key, 12*d*. whether they shod a courser or a carthorse, and a thousand nails for 18*d*. They had to have a distinctive mark on their horseshoes. In 1601, the Blacksmiths, Lockers, Whitesmiths, Farriers, Troogers—makers of wooden baskets—Turners and Cutlers were incorporated in a single mystery.

Essentially, the guild had a religious basis, and in the smaller towns, where there were no trade guilds, a religious fraternity might take their place. The trade or craft guild proper was a combination of trade association, trade union and benefit society, regulating the custom and guarding the reputation of its trade, governing apprenticeship, examining the qualifications of the finished apprentice, defending the rights of the trade, and administering charities. Sometimes, as in France, certain crafts were limited in numbers or hereditary. The guild of smiths at Newcastle-on-Tyne evidenced the bitter feeling between the folk immediately south of the border and the Scots—a feeling which has left some faint echoes behind—by forbidding its members to take a Scotsman as apprentice or workman.

Despite the fact that the guilds were usually jealous of the fair name of their crafts, the Smiths' Guild at Coventry was in trouble with the municipal authorities in 1436, when the attention of the leet was drawn to certain malpractices which had arisen among the ironworkers. Certain workers in iron, it was alleged, by employing labourers of the four allied crafts of smiths, brakemen, girdlers and card wire-drawers, had acquired complete control over the trade and were able to pass off inferior and ill-wrought iron upon their customers. It was suggested that a master should be allowed to employ only labourers of two of these occupations, instead of four, in the future—the smiths and brakemen to be linked together and the girdlers and card wire-drawers.

If, then, it was urged, the card wire-drawer, who made combs for combing wool, was "deceived" by his supplier, the smith, he would say to the latter, "Sir, I hadde of you late badde wire, sir, amend your honde, or in feithe I will no more bye of you." Then the smith, "lest he lose his customers, wold made true goode; and then with the grase of God the craft shuld amend and the kinges peapull not disseyved with contrewe goode". The burden of the charge seems to lie in the effect on the trade of the user of the iron goods. Eventually, agreement was reached and the master-smiths agreed to employ only journeymen who were smiths and brakemen.[1]

Naturally enough, perhaps, the guilds of Smiths proper, working in iron, were not among the wealthier and more aristocratic of the guilds, but the Smiths' Guild at Canterbury is recorded as holding land as late as 1660, despite the reduction in the wealth of such fraternities in general consequent upon the Reformation. In the seventeenth century, many of the City Companies were engaged in extensive financial operations, and the Farriers' Company, founded in 1356, then made a demise to their Clerk of his dwelling in the hall, on condition that he would assist in raising monies for the Company when needful and would be co-security, with the wardens and assistants. He was also bound in £50 to continue in their service. In the reign of Elizabeth, the Smiths and Cutlers of Hereford, owing to a scarcity of sea-coal, had presented a petition to the Mayor against forestallers and "regraters", and were influential

[1] *Mediaeval Towns: Coventry* (Mary D. Harris).

enough to get an ordinance passed forbidding the general
public to buy coal until after twelve noon.

The guilds, as representative bodies and closely connected
with municipal administration, took their part in the provision
of the Watch and in the great procession of the Watch at Mid-
summer and St. Peter's Eves. In London, in 1518, the Companies keeping the Watch included the Cutlers, Girdlers, and
Armourers, each providing four men: the Blacksmiths and the
Spurriers only provided two apiece. At Winchester, however, in
the Corpus Christi procession, the Smiths and Barbers, united,
took second place only to the Carpenters and Felters, in 1435.
In the Watch procession at Coventry, the guilds all paraded in
their liveries and some of the crafts provided armed men, the
Smiths hiring four. There, too, the Smiths had a chapel in
St. Michael's Church and took a prominent part in the presenta-
tion of the miracle plays.

When the Church itself gave up presenting miracle plays
in the churches, and the "pageants" went out into the streets,
it was a natural thing for the guilds, with their religious
affinities and their organization, to take charge of the presentation of the "mysteries", just as today group organizations of
one kind or another will take the responsibility for portions of
a procession, a carnival or a festival, hold stalls at a bazaar,
or stage displays at an exhibition. The guilds were, in most
countries of Western Europe, the most active, and in some
cases no doubt the only, corporate organizations existing in a
city or borough, often indeed controlling the civic government
itself. To them, therefore, was deputed, throughout the Middle
Ages, the responsibility for staging the various scenes at a
"mystery" play, each scene being put under the charge of a
guild, or perhaps a group of guilds, responsible, year by year,
for its presentation, its casting and the maintenance of properties, including the "pageant", a movable platform constituting
the stage.

Usually, where there was any possibility of relating the craft
to the scene, it seems to have been done, judging from some
marked examples and from the fact that, in various places, a
craft may be found to be presenting the same or a similar
scene, obviously because of some apparent or obscure appropriateness. Thus, the Cooks, at Chester, did the "Harrowing of

Hell", with appropriate fieriness in the scene, and the Water Carriers the Flood, while at York the Tylers or Thatchers did the manger scene, the Shipwrights the building of the Ark, the Fishmongers and Mariners the scene in the Ark, the Chandlers the Star in the East—no doubt with plenty of candles—the Vintners Christ turning the water into wine.

The Smiths in the Hereford plays presented "Longys and his knights", the soldiers of the Crucifixion, and not far away, in the more famous cycle at Coventry, the Smiths had the "Pageant of the Trial, Condemnation and Crucifixion of Christ", between the years 1447 and 1585. Possibly the underlying appropriateness laid, in this case, in the provision of the nails, the tools and the weapons—or there might have been in mind the ancient legend as to the four nails which the Smiths of Jerusalem were called upon to make for the Crucifixion—told elsewhere in this book. Armour and weapons may have had something to do with the Norwich Smiths doing "David and Goliath."

It is difficult, however, to see the relationship in the presentation of "Jesus being tempted" by the Fevers or Smiths of York, "Christ in the Temple" by the Smiths of Chester, or in the Cutlers and Bladesmiths presenting Judas selling Jesus—unless there was some reflection on the ethics of the craft, which would hardly have been accepted with complacency by its members! The pageant of the Three Kings, with their gifts, was an obvious allocation for the Goldsmiths, but at Chester they had the Killing of the Innocents. At Chester, too, the Blacksmiths, very intriguingly, had the Pageant of the Purification. Was there any conscious thought there of the world-wide and age-old quality of purifying associated with the fire? There is a curious, though possibly accidental, combination of the dual functions of primitive smiths in relation to war and agriculture in the assignment to the Armourers of the Pageant in which the angel, in the Garden of Eden, gives the guilty pair a spade with which to dig.

The pageants were guarded in their passage from point to point in the town by an escort provided by the guild concerned, and in 1476 the Company of Armourers ordered that

"all the masters of the same craft from now furth yearly, on Corpus Christi day, in the morning, be ready in their own proper persons, every one of them with an honest weapon, to await upon their pageant masters and pageant, at the first place where they shall begin. And so to await upon the same their pageant through the city, to the play be played as of that same pageant",

a regulation copied by the Spurriers and Loriners in 1493. In 1490, the Coventry Smiths paid 1s. 2d. for having their pageant moved from place to place.[1]

Once a play was allotted to a guild it was bound, under penalty, worthily to produce it, but sometimes the guild concerned, if it was not a wealthy one, was helped by contributions from guilds not themselves having the responsibility of a Pageant of their own. At Coventry, the Smiths were assisted by a contribution which the Bakers, Chandlers and Cooks were ordered to make towards the expenses of the Trial and Crucifixion of Christ. Even so, the Smiths seemed to have failed or faltered in their obligations in the matter, as in 1428 they were ordered to "occupie the said parchand for the evry yere upon the payne of xl" (£10) "to be payed at evry defaute to the use of the chamber". A yearly rate for the expenses was levied on every guild member, varying from 1d. to 4d.[2]

While the guild was responsible for providing the players, they were not necessarily guild members and were paid for their services, payment being according to the length of the part rather than its importance, and ranging generally from a few pence to 4s., plus liberal refreshments. Where a player doubled parts, he was paid accordingly; the Coventry Smiths, in 1584, paid Reginald Headly 5s. for playing Symon and Phyneas, John Hopper 3s. for playing Jesus and Zacharias, and John Green 2s. for two parts. There were no highly paid "stars" making fleeting appearances in the caste! In 1452, the Coventry Smiths, obviously still finding difficulty in presenting their pageant, contracted out with one Thomas Colchow to present it for them for the next twelve years, at an emolument of 46s. 8d., the craft, however, finding the pageant, clothes and rushes.[3]

The Coventry Smiths have left a detailed account of some

---

[1] *The Miracle Play in England* (S. W. Clarke).
[2] Ibid.
[3] Ibid.

A Tudor smith: carving on a house in Ipswich

of their expenses. In 1584, supper for the players at the close
of the day cost 8s. 6d.—at a time when a gallon of ale cost 2d.,
a quart of wine 2d., and a goose 4d. or less. The expenses of the
first rehearsal of the Smiths' pageant in Easter week, 1490, are
given as

Bread	4d.
Ale	8d.
"Kitchen"	13d.
Vinegar	1d.

At the second rehearsal, in Whitsun week, the cost, in
bread, ale and "kechyn", is given as 2s. 4d.

Other expenses recorded are

1462. Repairs to the "pageant": a pair of new wheels,
8s. Nails and two hooks, 4d.

1470. Iron clamps, 8d., two legs for the pageant and
workmanship, 7d.

1480. Two pairs of new wheels, 8s. Expenses putting
them on, 7d. Binding them, 8d. Paid to a carpenter for the pageant roof, 6d.

1499. Paid for having the pageant out, sweeping it,
putting it back, and for nails and two clasps of
iron and mending a broken clasp, and "for
coterellis and for a bordor to the pagaunte", 19d.

1554. Painting the pageant top, 22d.

Also, mending the pageant doors, 4d., for a key and setting
on the lock on the door, 5d., half-year's rent of the pageant-
house, 2s. 6d., given to Bryan, a "sharman", for his good will
of the pageant-house, 10d.

In 1587, shortly after the attempted revival of the Coventry
plays, which were in abeyance from 1580 to 1584,[1] the Smiths
sold their pageant-house for a pound, and the pageant itself for
40s. Other properties used by the Coventry Smiths between
1449 and 1585 are listed as

The Cross with a Rope to draw it up and a Curtain
hanging before it.
Gilding for the Pillar and the Cross.

[1] At the revival in 1584, a new scene on the Destruction of Jerusalem was
added—the author being an Oxford scholar named *Smythe*.

2 Pair of Gallows.

4 Scourges and a Pillar.

Scaffold.

Fanes to the Pageant.

(Mending of Imagery is mentioned in 1469.)

A Standard of red Buckram.

Two red Pensiles of Cloth painted and silk Fringe.

Iron to hold up the Streamer.

4 Gowns and 4 Hoods for the Tormentors (later described
as Jackets of black buckram with nails and dice
upon them). Other 4 gowns with damask flowers;
also 2 jackets, party red and black.

2 Mitres, for Caiaphas and Annas.

A Rochet for one of the Bishops.

God's Coat of white leather, 6 skins.

A Staff for the Demon.

2 Spears.

Gloves (12 pair).

Herod's Crest of Iron.

Scarlet Hoods and a Tabard.

Hats and Caps.

Cheverel (Wig) for God.

3 Cheverels and a Beard.

2 Cheverels gilt for Jesus and Peter.

Faulchion for Herod.

Scarlet Gown.

Maces.

In 1591, the whole series was put out to contract by the Coventry guilds, but that was the last performance.

The echoes of the mystery plays still sound in the Oberammergau Passion Play. In 1950, a blacksmith, Hugo Rutz, played the part of Peter.

Another echo of the Middle Ages may sometimes be found in old towns, where streets may carry names telling of the crafts which once made them their quarter—a practice still to be found in the East. In the mediaeval town of Hall, in Tirol, there are still two working smithies in Schmied Street, and at one of them the author witnessed a cow being shod, in 1950.

CHAPTER XII

THE POST-MEDIAEVAL SMITH

An Ode on Smithery, 1610

By reading of old authors we do find
The smiths have been a trade time out of mind;
And it's believed they may be bold to say,
There's not the like to them now at this day.
For was it not for smiths what could we do,
We soon should lose our lives and money too;
The miser would be stript of all his store,
And lose the golden god he doth adore:
No tradesman could be safe or take his rest
But thieves and rogues would nightly him molest;
It's by our cunning art, and ancient skill,
That we are saved from those who would work ill.
The smith at night, and soon as he doth rise,
Doth always cleanse and wash his face and eyes;
Kindles his fire, and the bellows blows,
Tucks up his shirt sleeves, and to work he goes;
Then makes the hammer and the anvil ring,
And thus he lives as merry as a king.
A working smith all other trades excels,
In useful labour wheresoe'er he dwells;
Toss up your caps ye sons of Vulcan then,
For there are none of all the sons of men,
That can with the brave working smiths compare,
Their work is hard, and jolly lads they are.
What though a smith looks sometimes very black,
And sometimes gets but one shirt to his back
And that is out at elbows, and so thin
That you through twenty holes may see his skin;
Yet when he's drest and clean, you all will say,
That smiths are men not made of common clay.
They serve the living, and they serve the dead,
They serve the mitre and the crownèd head;
They all are men of honour and renown,
Honest and just, and loyal to the crown.
The many worthy deeds that they have done,

Have spread their fame beyond the rising sun,
So if we have offended rich or poor,
We will be good boys, and do so no more.
                    From *Hone's Everyday Book* (1826?)

ACTUALLY, there seems to be no evidence of the accuracy of
the dating of the doggerel verse quoted at the head of this
chapter; the correspondent who supplied it to the *Everyday
Book*, in 1825, refers to it as having been recited by an old man
in his day, and the wording seems rather later than the seventeenth century. Nevertheless, the picture is true enough of that
period or a later one. There is little of mythical romance or
colour about the post-mediaeval smith, save for the rather
artificial romance woven around Gretna Green in the eighteenth
and early nineteenth centuries. No longer do we hear of
wonderful swordsmiths, of smiths who were magicians or
warriors, of the guildsman playing his part in the mystery plays,
or the artisan distinguished from other workers by the freedom
won by his skill and craftsmanship.

The rural blacksmith, in general, becomes just another
rustic, while the town smith has become goldsmith, armourer,
locksmith, and many another special craftsman who has left
behind and looks down upon the grimy forge and "elementary"
work of the blacksmith. Even the ironworking services of the
latter are circumscribed compared with his versatility of the
earlier periods, and the ornamental work of the church door,
the grille around the tomb or the gate of the manor house often
—not always—came from ironworking centres or were even
imported, especially from Flanders. The supremacy of wrought
ironwork, too, was being challenged, especially where the
furniture of the hearth was concerned, by cast-iron products,
made in the foundries from patterns and so dispensing with the
handicraft of the rural smith.

At this time, the Wealden iron industry of Sussex, Kent and
East Hampshire was in full blast, leaving behind it names
redolent of ferrous industry—Cold Ash, Hammer, Hammervale,
Hammer Bottom. Further west, iron casting was being done
at Bishops Waltham, and at Boldre in the New Forest, where
a plentiful supply of charcoal was to be had, iron from Hengist-
bury Head was smelted, and the still existing pond at Sowley
was used to drive a huge hammer for forging.

On the other hand, the English blacksmith was an integral and necessary part of rural life; the multiplication of amenities and the development of the domestic hearth increased the number of household implements which the smith could be expected to make or repair, in addition to the growing demand for agricultural implements.

In 1678, Joseph Moxon wrote, in his *Mechanick Exercises*, "Smithing is an Art Manual, by which an irregular Lump, or several Lumps, of Iron is wrought to an intended Shape." The forge of his time he described as usually having a brick base, 2 ft. 6 in. or 2 ft. 9 in. high, with hollow arches under, and furnished with an iron hood and chimney, and with a bellows worked by a lever rod. It is interesting to note the descent from the domestic hearth here: the arched pediment coming from the Roman cooking range, and the hood from the fireplace of the thirteenth century. Moxon lists as tools the anvil, tongs, hammer, sledge, vice, hand-vice, pliers, drill, drill-bow, the screw-plate and its taps: mostly the elementary tools of the smiths of all ages. Discussing the "Several heats Smiths take of their Iron", he observes that "Blood-red Heat" is to be used when the iron has already assumed its final form but needs a little hammering to smooth it; "Flame or White Heat" when iron has to be forged into its form and size; and "Sparkling or Welding Heat" only when you are doubling up two bars or pieces of iron to make them into one piece or making several bars into one.

Brazing and soldering, he says, are only employed by smiths where work is too thin or small to be welded. Moxon goes on to state that English iron is mostly coarse, hard and brittle, chiefly suitable for fire-bars, etc., unless it comes from the Forest of Dean or "some few places more". Swedish iron is the best used in England, and Spanish would be as good, but that it is liable to "crack betwixt hot and cold". It is also unevenly wrought in the bars, "so costs a good deal for smoothing, but is suitable for anvils, sledges and hammers". "Dort Squares", imported from Holland but made in Germany, is only suitable for window-bars, fire-bars, etc.

English steel is made in several places, such as Yorkshire, Gloucestershire, Sussex, the Weald of Kent, but the best is made about the Forest of Dean; it breaks fiery, with a somewhat coarse grain, but if well wrought it makes good edge tools, files and punches. "Flemish" steel, also made in Germany, is used for watch-springs, punches and file-cutters' chisels: it breaks with a fine grain, works well at the forge and will take a welding heat. Spanish steel is too brittle for springs or punches, but makes good fine-edged tools. So-called Swedish steel resembles Flemish, "Venice steel" is chiefly used for razors and surgical instruments. He refers to the making of hinges, locks, screws, nuts and keys. Describing the twisting of iron, an important point in the ornamental smithing of the periods, he says:

"Squares and flat bars, sometimes are by smiths, Twisted for Ornament. It is very easily done; for after the Bar is square or flat-Forg'd (and if the curiosity of your work require it truly Fil'd) you must take a Flame-heat, or if your Work be small, but Blood-red heat, and you may twist it about, as much or as little as you please, either with the Tongs, Vice, or Hand-vice. . . ."[1]

Generally, however, the smith of old England was portrayed in the telling epitaph of Thomas Pierce:

Here Lyeth Thomas pierce, whom no man taught,
Yet he in Iron, Brass and Silver wrought.
Died Feb, 1635. A.D. aet. 77.

Celia Fiennes, in her travels, at the end of the seventeenth century, recognized that, if the smith was a craftsman whom "no man taught", he was indeed taught by experience and his own intelligence. She complained that, in the Lake District,

"these stony hills and wayes pulls off a shooe presently and wear them so thin that it was a constant charge to shooe my horses every two or three days; but this smith did shooe them so well and so good shooes that they held some of the shooes six weeks; the stonyness of the wayves all here about teaches them the art of making good shooes and setting them on fast".

[1] Quoted in Briggs' *Short History of the Building Crafts.*

There is a world of common sense and a moral of widespread application in the good lady's keen observation!

The rural blacksmith, too, had to be a man of many parts. Even in his ordinary line of farriery, he had to be much more than a shoer of horses. Often, he had to be "vet" as well, in days when scientific veterinary surgery was unknown; just as the gypsy blacksmith of east and southern Europe today usually combines with his smithcraft an expert knowledge of horses. Like the "barber-surgeon", he was the pioneer of what is today a separate and learned profession.[1] Markham, in 1622, referred to "an excellent Smith or Farrier: who shall ever be furnished with Horse-shoes, Nayles and drugges, both for inward and outward applications". His only competitor in this respect would be the charlatan "horse-coper".

Of such men, the authors of *Old English Household Life*[2] write:

"if a rushlight holder or any single implement for the house was wanted, or a hoe for field or garden, it was made by the nearest smith. The men who shaped the rainwater heads in lead, forged the firedogs, wrought the panelling or erected stone or brickwork at the country houses and halls, belonged to the villages. They also supplied themselves and their neighbours at the farms and houses and cottages, producing all manner of necessities for the homes and the fields."

Even clockmaking and repairing was a branch of the blacksmith's work well into the seventeenth century. *The House and Farm Accounts of W. Shuttleworth* (Chetham Society) show entries:

1578. ". . . whereas Thomas Hall, blacksmythe, has the greatest pte of a clock of myne . . .
1597. ". . . the smith at Lostoke for working one day at the cloke at Smithelles . . . vjd."

while Robert Smith, of Poole, was paid the large sum of 6s. 8d. in 1532 for repairing the clock at the church of St. James, as

[1] The Royal Veterinary College was founded in 1791.
[2] *Old English Household Life* (Gertrude Jekyll and Sydney R. Jones).

well as, on another occasion, 1s. for making a candlestick to
stand in the window before St. Katharine, and for mending
a lock.[1]

At the beginning of the seventeenth century, there was a
colony of watch- and clockmakers in London, whose numbers
were sufficiently great in 1630 to secure a charter of incorporation for their Livery Company, but scattered about the countryside were blacksmith clockmakers, who made and repaired the
large clocks,[2] such as graced the village church towers. The
Churchwardens' Accounts for Yarnton Church, Oxfordshire,
contain an entry for 1651:

> A pond of wire for the clock   1s. 4d.
> The smith's boy for coming over to mend it   3s. 8d.

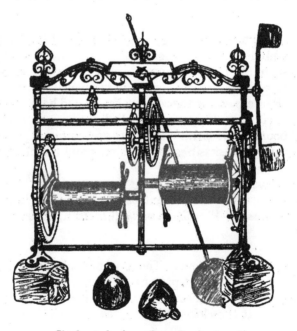

Clock works from Bere Regis church,
'Lawrence Boyce, Puddletown, *fecit*, 1719'

[1] *History of Poole* (H. P. Smith).
[2] *A Book of English Clocks* (R. W. Symonds).

He must have taken some time over it, though, or come a long distance, for the blacksmith employed on Berwick Bridge in 1634 was only paid 8*d*. a day—and that was 2*d*. more than the smith of Lostock had in 1597! In that same year, 1651, Wigan church clock was mended by William Harvey, who was a Warden of the Blacksmiths' Company there.

Tompion, 1639–1713, probably the best-known English clockmaker of all time, started his career as a blacksmith in Buckinghamshire, and even in the eighteenth century many of the parish church clocks were made by village smiths—some, indeed, in the nineteenth century, too. The works of the parish church clock from Bere Regis, inscribed "Lawrence Boyce, Puddletown, *fecit*, 1719", are to be seen in Dorchester Museum, and others are still in the church towers.

CHAPTER XIII

THE SMITH AND THE DEVIL

> Who hath formed a god or molten a graven image
> that is profitable for nothing? . . .
> The smith with the tongs both worketh in the coals
> and fashioneth it with hammers, and worketh it with the
> strength of his arms: yea, he is hungry, and his strength
> faileth: he drinketh no water and is faint. . . .
>
> Isaiah xliv.

AS THE author of this book remarked in his *Story of the Bridge*,
having regard to the reputation for craftiness given to the Evil
One, it is remarkable how often he is outwitted in folklore
stories.

Miss Dora Yates records a story of this kind in her *Book of
Gypsy Folk Tales*, as told by a Welsh gypsy.[1]

There was an old blacksmith who lived on the hill with his
wife and his mother-in-law, and the only work he could do
was to make ploughshares. The mother-in-law had an old mare.
Once there came to him a youth on horseback. "I want thee to
shoe my horse." "I cannot," quoth the old smith. "Then give
me the tools: I will do it."

The boy went off and made a great fire. He came out and
cut the horse's four legs off. He staunched the blood and put
the four legs on the fire. He blew the fire a great while. He took
the four legs out of the fire, put them on the anvil, beat them
a great while, and threw them down. Then he picked them up,
and went out, and put them back under the horse. The old
smith was watching him. The youth asked what he had to pay
and gave the smith a golden guinea.

Some days afterwards the smith remembered about his
mother-in-law's mare. He wanted her shod. So away he went
and brought her to the smithy. He tied her to the door and
cut off the four legs and let them bleed. But he did not know

---

[1] The author is greatly indebted to Miss Yates and the Gypsy Lore Society,
in whose Journal it first appeared, for permission to reproduce this story in full.

how to staunch the blood. He went in and made a great fire and put the four legs on the fire. He blew and blew. Then he went to look for the legs. There was nothing to be seen: he had burnt them all to ashes. He took the old mare and threw her over the hedge.

The mother-in-law and her daughter were always quarrelling. The old smith did not know what to do with them. In a day or two the youth on horseback returned with two old women. "Canst thou make these two old women young?" he asked. "No, I cannot." "Wilt lend me thy tools? I will do it." "Yes, take them."

The youth got off his horse; he flung down the two old women and bound them. He made a great fire and put them on the fire. He blew and he blew beneath them. Then he took them outside, set them on the anvil, hammered them well and set them down. They became two young and beautiful ladies. The old smith was watching the youth. The boy gave him a golden guinea.

A few days afterwards it occurred to the smith to do the same with his wife and his mother-in-law. He took the twain and bound them, and set them on the fire. And he blew and he blew beneath them. Then he went to look for them. There was nothing to be seen: they were burnt to ashes. He flung down the hammer, and went out. "I have done it now! I have killed my old mare and I have killed my wife and my mother-in-law." He scratched his head and knew not what to do. So he left the smithy and set forth in deep snow and wind, and he had never a hat on his head. The young boy followed him and asked, "Shall I come with thee?" "No," quoth the smith, "thou hast naught to do with me." "Do let me come with thee." The old smith took him. The boy was barefoot. The boy talked to him. "Near by is a great castle, and in it is a mighty lord. He is ill in bed. Let us go there." "I can do nothing," quoth the smith. "Say naught then: we will go there together and I will do everything. Tell them that I am thy servant."

Down they went to the castle and knocked at the door. The butler came out. "We have come here to heal the great lord." "Come in!" He took them in to sit by the fire. He asked them what they would have to eat and drink. They got plenty to eat and drink. The old smith forgot what they had to do. The little boy said to him, "Now then, when the butler comes in, say that thou wishest to go to the lord."

They went up to the lord. The young boy called for a knife, a pot, water and a spoon. He cut off the lord's head and spat on his hands to staunch the blood. He put the head in the pot, and set it on the fire to boil. It boiled a great while. He took a golden spoon and stirred it with the spoon. He took the head out of the pot and put it back on the lord's neck. The lord got well and stood up. The lord gave them a sack of gold and they set off along the road. "All that I want," quoth the little boy, "is new shoes." "No, I cannot give thee any: there is little enough for myself," quoth the smith. The little boy went off and left him.

The old smith went on alone. He met two men on horseback and they seized all his money. The smith journeyed on. He heard about a great castle, and that the lord of the castle was ill. Up goes the smith to see him. He knocked at the door. The butler called him in and gave him plenty to eat. After he had done eating, the old smith went up to see the lord. He called for a pot and water and a spoon. He cut off the lord's head and let it bleed, but he did not know how to staunch the blood. He put the head in the pot on the fire to boil: it boiled a great while. He took the spoon and stirred it. He could do nothing to it; the head was falling to pieces and the lord was bleeding to death.

Someone came and knocked at the door. The smith was afraid. "No one must come in here." "Wilt thou let the little barefoot boy in?" The old smith hearkened and opened the door, and let the little boy come in. He walked straight up to the lord and staunched the blood. Then he went to the pot, took a golden spoon and stirred the head. It was a great while before he could get the head together again: it was boiled to rags. He took it out and set it on the lord's neck. The lord sat up. The smith and the little boy went away after getting two sacks of gold.

On the road the boy begged, "I want shoes." "Very well," said the smith, "all the money is thine." The boy said, "I do not want it: I want shoes." The boy got his shoes.

The two were walking along the road, and the little boy said: "There is another great lord who lives near by. This lord has a wizard and no one can beat him. Let us go there. There are three sacks of gold to be won, if we beat him."

They went up to the door to get speech with the lord. They were given food and came away. Then they went into an old house, where there was a huge pair of bellows. The lord's wizard blew up half the sea. "Now it is thy turn, little boy," said the smith. The boy began to blow. He blew up a great fish that drank all the sea. The wizard began to blow again. He blew up corn like rain. The little boy tried and he blew up birds that ate up all the corn. The lord's man blew up many rabbits. The little boy tried again and he blew three greyhounds and the greyhounds ate up the rabbits. He beat the lord's wizard; they got three sacks of gold.

The old smith hardly knew what to do with his money. It occurred to him to build a new smithy, and he built a few new houses, a workshop and three inns.

One day he was doing a little work when an old woman came to the door at nightfall to beg for a lodging. "All right," quoth the old smith, "I can give thee a bed for one night. I have no serving maid, so go into the house, put the kettle on the fire and make some tea for thyself." The old woman ate something and went to bed. In the morning she arose, and the old smith and she had breakfast together. "I will give thee three wishes—what dost thou desire?" quote the old woman. The smith said to her, "I wish that the man who takes my hammer in his hand cannot put it down again until I say so." He got his wish. "What is thy second wish?" quoth the old woman. "Dost thou see that old chair in the corner?" "Yes," quoth the old woman. "I wish that the man who seats himself there cannot get up again until I set him free." "All right! Thou shalt have thy desire." "And I wish that the man who gets into my pocket cannot get out again until I let him." "All right!" quoth the old woman. She thanked him and went her way.

A few days after, when his money had run low, a man came to the smithy. He asked the smith how he was. "Very well," quoth he, "how art thou?" They talked for some time until at last this man asked the smith whether he would sell himself. The smith considered a little. "Yes," quoth he, "how much money wilt thou give me?" "I will give thee a sack of gold." "Give it me," quoth the smith. "Thou must come away with

me in five years' time: I will return to fetch thee." The Evil
One departed and the smith went out to the inn to get a drink.

One day he was in the smithy doing a little work, when the
Evil One arrived. "Now thou must come away with me." "Very
well," said the smith. "Wait a moment, take my hammer and
do a little beating on this anvil. I will come back when I have
finished this small job."

The smith took his work home and afterwards went to one
of his inns. He did some hard drinking there, came out, and
went to the next inn. He had a drop there too and came out.
Lo! The Evil One leaves the forge, hammer in hand, and goes
to seek for the smith. He found him in the farthest inn drinking
with the gentry. In came the old Devil. The smith stood up.
"What art thou doing with my tools?" he asked. "Come here,"
quoth the Devil. "Remove this thing and I will give thee five
years more." The old smith took the hammer and went home.

The five years passed. . . . Just after they had come to
an end the Devil walked into the smithy. "How art thou?"
quoth he to the smith. "Very well! how art thou?" "Now thou
must come away with me." "All right! Sit down in that old
chair." The Devil sat down. "Wait there a moment," quoth the
smith, "I want to go home with this." The smith went off down
to the inn. He got half drunk. The old Devil was tired of sitting
down. He tried to get up, but could not. At last he walked off
with the old chair behind him down to the inn. He asked
whether the landlord was in. "No," quoth the woman, "he is
not here, he has gone to the next inn."

The Devil followed him to the second inn, and strode into
the parlour. And there he found the smith. He looked at the
Devil. "What is that man doing with my chair?" said he.
"Come here," quoth the Devil. "I want a word with thee. Take
away this chair and I will give thee five years more." The smith
dragged away the chair and the Devil departed. The smith
returned home.

The five years passed. . . . Lo! the old Devil is back again.
There was no one in the workshop: the smith was out drinking.
The old Devil went to seek for him. He found him in the
parlour. The old Devil sat down beside him, and whispered in
his ear. Said the smith: "I have called for ale. Turn thyself
into a pound in my pocket that I may pay for it." The Devil

did so. The old smith drank his fill and went home to bed. He was just falling asleep when something under his head began to cry out. He got up, came downstairs, went into the smithy, took the pocket, held it on the anvil, seized the hammer, and beat it soundly. "Let me go," quoth the old Devil, "and I will leave thee alone. I will never trouble thee again if thou wilt let me go now." The old smith let him go.

Then the smith died, and he went to the Devil's door and knocked. An imp of Satan came out. "Tell thy father that the smith is here." The little demon went and told his father. "Do not let him in," quoth the old Devil, "he will kill us all. Here!" quoth the old Devil to his serving-man, "take this wisp of straw and set fire to it to light him up to my dear God." The Devil's servant did so. The old smith went up to my dear God. There he sits playing the harp, and there we shall all see him one day, if we do not go to the Devil instead.

.   .   .   .   .

From Flanders there comes a very detailed folklore story in similar vein, undoubtedly with the same ultimate origin, but given an anti-Spanish, anti-Catholic, politico-religious turn. Smetse Smee, a smith of Ghent, farrier, armourer and agricultural engineer, so prosperous that he had four assistants, had his business undermined by an unscrupulous rival, who won the support of, and truckled to, the Spaniards and those who opposed the reformed faith, until, emboldened by drink, Smee avenged himself by throwing his rival into the river, where he became entangled with a dead dog! Still, however, Smetse's business dwindled until, on the verge of committing suicide, he is persuaded to sell himself to the Evil One, as the price of renewed prosperity for seven years.

Despite the misgivings and protests of his wife, wealth and good things were showered upon him, usually by night; his assistants returned to work and the smithy was enlarged; though doing good with his wealth, the smith was no longer Smetse the Merry, but only Smetse the Rich—and he counted the days. On the twenty-fourth day of the seventh year, there came a ragged wayfarer to the forge, with an ass, a sweet wife, and a little child—Joseph, Mary and Jesus—poor and needy.

Despite his compact, the smith retained his faith, and three boons were granted to him—that whoever climbed a certain plum tree in his garden should not be able to come down again, that whoever sat in a certain chair should not be able to rise, and that whoever got into a sack should not be able to get out again, until the smith desired. Holding cheerfully to his new secret, the smith awaited the coming of the end of the seven years, and the visit of the Devil in the guise of the ghost of an erstwhile persecutor of heretics.

It took some manœuvring to get the Satanic emissary into the plum tree, but there, beaten first by sticks, and then by the smith's assistants armed with hammers and iron bars, he eventually conceded Smetse another seven years. The second messenger came in the form of the Duke D'Alva. It took nine workmen—Smetse's staff had evidently increased—to bring the magic chair, in which, helpless but proud, the bloody Duke was beaten and reminded of his cruel deeds, until, humbled and resentful, he added another seven years of grace.

More and more frightened the poor smith's wife became, more and more masses she offered, until, twenty-one years after the signing of the black compact, there came, heralded by lice and an evil stench, no less a person that Philip II of Spain. To him, tortured by the lice, Smetse told how, by the advice of St. Joseph, he had been cured of a similar plague by getting into the sack. This time, beaten to a mass of a hotch-potch of bones and flesh, the royal devil could only purchase release by the complete surrender of the fatal deed. Mrs. Smetse, however, made sure of the release by sprinkling all the tools of prosperity with holy water. The legend concludes with a vision of Hell, Smetse's return to poverty and his passage through Purgatory.

In this version, too, the door of Hell is slammed in his face, with fear at his tricks on the diabolical messengers, yet he was forbidden entry into Paradise for his conduct in making terms with the Devil, until he was brought by two or three halberdier (!) angels into the presence of My Lord Jesus Himself, who, after ascertaining he had fought and suffered for freedom of conscience, showed charity even to his rival, but above all soundly thrashed the ghosts of Jacob Hessels, the Duke of Alva and King Philip II of Spain, gave him leave to enter!

Smithy, St. Lawrence, Jersey, with cage for shoeing horses in the
background—tiring platform in foreground

"Balling iron" from a Taunton smithy

G. Elmes & Son's smithy, Wareham, Dorset. Cow horn on the bellows lever

With so many gypsy tales, there are echoes of an older folklore, suggesting that the gypsies were not so much inventors of stories as adapters of folk-tales they picked up in their wanderings. In the miraculous shoeing of the horse we have, of course, an echo of the unorthodox shoeing exploit of St. Eloi. An even closer parallel to the gypsy story occurs in a Norse tale,[1] "The Master Smith". In this, the smith had made a bargain with the Archfiend that the latter should have him after seven years, but during that time he was to be the Master of his craft. So, over the forge was a notice, "Here dwells The Master over all Masters." Our Lord and St. Peter, passing by, saw the notice, and our Lord entered the smithy. "Who are you?" he said to the smith, who replied, "Read what's written over the door, but maybe you can't read writing. If so, you must wait till someone comes to help you."

At that point, a man entered with a horse to be shod, and our Lord asked leave to shoe it. "You may try, if you like," said the smith, "you can't do it so badly that I shall not be able to make it right again." So our Lord took each leg off the horse, one by one, laid it in the fire and made the shoe red-hot, after which he turned up the ends of the shoe and filed down the heads of the nails and clenched the points; then he put back the leg on the horse again.[2] "You're not so bad a smith after all," said the smith.

Then came the smith's mother to call him to dinner—an old woman with an ugly crook on her back and wrinkles in her face. So our Lord laid her in the fire and smithied a lovely young woman out of her. After dinner, the smith, having a horse to shoe, tried to do as our Lord had done, but the legs burnt to ashes and he had to pay for the horse. Undaunted, he seized an old beggar woman, and despite her entreaties, put her on the fire—but no lovely maiden emerged. Rebuked for her death by our Lord, the smith replied, "There's not many who'll ask after her, I'll be bound; but it's a shame of the Devil if this is the way he holds what is written up over the door."

Given, for some unexplained reason, the option of three

---

[1] *Tales from the Norse* (Sir G. W. Dasent).
[2] A variant of the St. Eloi legend makes the saint the smith who put up he boastful notice, Our Lord, as a youth, the miraculous smith, and St. eorge the owner of the horse; after failing to perform the miracle in imitation, t. Eloi was supposed to have destroyed his signboard.

H

wishes, the smith wished, first, that anyone he asked to climb into the pear tree that stood outside the forge might stay sitting there until he asked him to come down, secondly that anyone he asked to sit in his easy chair inside the workshop should remain there until he asked him to get up, and last that anyone he should ask to creep into the steel purse in his pocket might stay in it until the smith gave him leave to creep out again. "You have wished as a wicked man," said St. Peter; "first and foremost you should have wished for God's grace and good will." "I dursn't look so high as that," said the smith, so our Lord and St. Peter took their leave.

The years went by, and the Devil came for the price of the bargain. "Oh," said the smith, "I must just hammer the head of this tenpenny nail first; meantime you can just climb up into the pear tree and pluck yourself a pear to gnaw at; you must be both hungry and thirsty after your journey." The Devil did so—and was only released on promising not to come back for four years. Then the smith wanted time to sharpen the point, while the Devil rested in the easy chair; thus, despite persuasion and anger on the Evil One's part, a further delay of four years was wrung from him. At the end of the second four years, the smith agreed to go, but first, he must know if the Devil could make himself as small as he pleased. So, he was got into the purse.

With that, the smith laid the purse in the fire and made it red-hot; taking his sledge-hammer he let fly with such purpose as to get a promise from the Devil never to come near him again. "Very well," said the smith, "now I think the links are pretty well welded and you may come out," so he unclasped the purse and away went the Devil in such a hurry that he didn't once look behind him. After this, it occurred to the smith that, having thrown away his chance of entering the Kingdom of Heaven, he had better make friends with the Devil again, or he would not get in to Hell either—but when he arrived at the gates of Hell, and the Devil heard who it was, the fiend charged the watch to go back and lock up all the nine locks on Hell's gates. "And," said he, "you may as well put on a padlock, for if he only once gets in he will turn Hell topsy-turvy."

In another Norse story, "The Lad and the De'il", a lad

walking along a road cracking nuts found one that was worm-eaten, just as he encountered the Devil. "Is it true, now," asked the lad, "what they say, that the De'il can make himself as small as he chooses, and thrust himself in through a pinhole?" The De'il assured him it was perfectly true, and, challenged to do it, entered the nut and was promptly trapped by the lad, who walked on to a smithy and asked the smith to crack a nut for him.

"Aye, that'll be an easy job," said the smith, and took his smallest hammer, laid the nut on the anvil, and gave it a blow, but it would not break. It was the same story with a bigger and yet a bigger hammer, so the smith got angry and seized his great sledge-hammer.

"Now, I'll crack you to bits," he said, and let drive at the nut with might and main. And so the nut flew to pieces with a bang that blew off half the roof of the smithy and the whole house creaked and groaned as though it were ready to fall.

"Why, if I don't think the De'il must have been in that nut," said the smith.

"So he was; you're quite right," said the lad.

.   .   .   .   .

The Devil, however, was not always defeated. In a Russian folk story of a smith and a demon, the smith was so impressed by a picture of the Devil in Hell that he had one painted on his smithy door. Every morning he would say a respectful "Good morrow" to the painting, and all went well until he died. Then his son, who took over the smithy, was not so respectful, but hit and kicked the demon each day. Here the old animist belief, that everything had its spirit, comes in, for the painted demon, resenting the treatment, came to life and got himself engaged as the young smith's apprentice. One day the seigneur's wife, old and unprepossessing, came to the smithy while the smith was absent and succumbed to the apprentice's assurances that he could make her young and beautiful in the forge—which he did. Soon afterwards, her husband, fearful of what might happen with his wife so much more youthful than himself, hastened to the smith and demanded that he, too, should be rejuvenated. In vain the smith protested his inability. (Alas, women can get away with a lot that men cannot; indeed, there is an old French saying, *"Ce que diable ne peut, femme le fait!"*) Finally, hard-pressed, the smith agreed to try the experiment, but only succeeded in burning the seigneur to a cinder. Justice does not recognize good intentions in such cases, and the smith would have been hanged, but for the opportune intervention of the demon apprentice, who, in return for a promise of better treatment in future, produced the seigneur alive and saved the smith.

There seems to be a pagan origin for this story; a Christian version would surely have discomfited the Devil, somehow or other!

CHAPTER XIV

PETULENGRO, THE GYPSY-SMITH

I am in a dingle, making a petul; and I must here observe that whilst I am making a horse-shoe the reader need not be surprised if I speak occasionally in the language of the horse-shoe . . . I have for some time past been plying the peshota, or bellows, endeavouring to raise up the yag, or fire, in my primitive forge. The angar, or coals, are now burning fiercely, casting forth sparks and long vagescoe chipes or tongues of flame; a small bar of sastra, or iron, is lying in the fire, to the length of ten or twelve inches and so far it is hot, very hot, exceeding hot, brother. And now you see me, prala, snatch the bar of iron and place the heated end of it upon the covantza or anvil, and forthwith I commence cooring the sastra as hard as if I had been engaged by a master at the rate of dui caulor or two shillings a day, brother; and when I have beaten the iron until it is nearly cool and my arm tired, I place it again in the angar and begin again to rouse the fire with the pudamengro, which signifies the blowing thing, and is another and more common word for bellows, and while thus employed I sing a gypsy song, the sound of which is wonderfully in unison with the hoarse moaning of the pudamengro, and ere the song is finished, the iron is again hot and malleable . . . I am in want of assistance; I want you, brother, to take the bar out of my hand and support it upon the covantza, whilst I am applying a chinomescro or sort of chisel to the heated iron and cut off, with a lusty stroke or two of the shukaro baro or big hammer, as much as required for the petul. . . . I place the piece in the fire and again apply the bellows and take up the song where I left it off, and, when I have finished the song, I take out the iron, but this time with my plaistra or pincers, and then I recommence hammering, turning the iron round and round with my pincers; and now I bend the iron, and lo, and behold, it has assumed something of the outline of a petul. . . . Having first well pared, with my churi, I applied each petul hot, glowing hot, to the pindro. Oh, how the hoofs hissed; and oh, the pleasant pungent odour

> which diffused through the dingle. . . . I shod the horse
> bravely, merely pricked him once with a cafi . . . and
> having finished the operation, I filed the hoof well with the
> rin baro (big file).
>
> GEORGE BORROW: *Lavengro.*

REFERENCE has already been made to the facts that early
smiths were frequently itinerant workers and that smiths
among many nations were of a special caste or even aliens to
the people for whom they worked. Both these conditions are
present with the gypsies, who have been metal workers for an
indefinite period—from the time, indeed, when they first come
into the daylight of history. Since it is now generally accepted
that their origin lies in India, it seems more than probable that
they were a race or caste of metal workers there who, for some
mysterious reason, were impelled to move westward, leaving,
as they came, pockets of alien and often despised metal workers,
such as the Haddad of the Arab world, and the Kauliyah of
Irak, who are blacksmiths and fiddlers, the Mutriba, makers of
swords, daggers, knives, iron implements and copper vessels,
and the Ganganah, blacksmiths, carpenters, burnishers and
makers of felt cloaks.[1]   .

Their status has always been a low one, partly perhaps
because of their inferior level of civilization or their, to Western
minds, criminal propensities, coupled with the fact that despite
lip service to religion they have generally been regarded as
pagans at heart. Legend has, however, woven a special reason
why the gypsy smith is an outcaste in the Christian world.

According to the version given by Konrad Bercovici, in his
Story of the Gypsies, when Jesus was given into the charge of
the jailers in readiness for His crucifixion, two Roman soldiers
were sent out to get four stout nails from some blacksmith.
But when the soldiers had set out with the money with which
to buy the nails, they first called at an inn, and spent half the
money on the wine that the Greeks sold in Jerusalem. It was
late in the afternoon when they remembered their errand again,
and they had to be back at the barracks by nightfall, for the
crucifixion was to take place the following morning. So they
left the inn hastily, hardly sober, and coming to the first smithy

[1] *The Story of the Gypsies* (Bercovici).

they summoned the blacksmith loudly, so as to frighten him into doing the work even if there was not enough money left to pay for it.

"Man, we want four big nails made right away to crucify Yeshua ben Miriam with; Yeshua ben Miriam, who has talked ill of our Emperor."

But the old Jewish blacksmith had seen Jesus when he had looked into the smithy and refused to make nails for his crucifixion, so one of the soldiers threw down the half of the money that was left and shouted:

"Here is money to pay for them. We speak in the name of the Emperor!" Then they held their lances close to the man but he still refused, so they ran him through, after setting his beard on fire.

It was getting late when they arrived at the next smithy. "Make us four stout nails," they demanded, "and we will pay you forty kreuzer for them."

"I can only forge four small nails for that price," said the man. But the soldiers showed him how large they wanted the nails.

The man shook his head. "I cannot make them for that price. I have a wife and children." "Jew," shouted the soldiers, "make us the nails and stop talking," and set his beard on fire. Frightened now, the Jew began to forge the nails, till one of the soldiers, helping at the forge, leaned over and told him they were wanted for the crucifixion of Jesus. The hand of the Jew remained poised high, with the hammer. Then the voice of the murdered smith called faintly to him: "Do not make the nails. They are for one of our people, an innocent man." So Aria dropped the hammer and refused to make the nails. "Make them," the soliders demanded, though frightened themselves also, for they had heard the voice. "Jew, you said you had a wife and children."

Meeting with a stubborn refusal, they ran him through too, and sought a third blacksmith, a Syrian. Scared by the bloody lances, he started to make the nails for the forty pieces, till the voices of the two murdered smiths called to him, when he too refused to make the nails and was killed. Night was near and the soldiers dared not return without the nails and half the money short, but outside the gates of the city they found a gypsy who had pitched his tent and set up his anvil. They ordered him to make the nails, and put the money down. Three nails had been made when, as the gypsy began to forge the fourth nail, the voices of the three murdered blacksmiths began to call.

Without waiting for the gypsy's reaction, the soldiers, with three nails in their possession, ran away, and the gypsy, with the money in his pocket, finished the fourth nail and waited for it to cool. He poured water on it, but it sizzled and the iron remained as hot as ever. More and more water—but the nail was glowing like a living, bleeding body and the blood was spurting fire. The nail glowed and glowed until a wide stretch of the darkened desert was illumined by its light. Terrified, the gypsy packed his tent and fled; tired, he pitched it again at midnight, far away—but there at his feet was the glowing nail he had left behind.

All night long he drew water from a nearby well and poured it on the nail, and when the water failed he threw sand on it, but still it glowed. Crazy with fear, the gypsy ran further into the desert and set up his tent at an Arab village, but the glowing nail still followed him. So, when an Arab came to him to join and patch the iron hoop of a wheel, he used the glowing nail, and directly afterwards fled onwards, until he reached Damascus and set up his forge there. Months later, a man brought the hilt of a sword to be repaired, but as the gypsy lit his forge the hilt began to glow from the iron of the nail on it, so he packed up and ran away yet again. It is said that that nail always appears in the tents of the descendants of the man who forged the nails for the crucifixion, and when the nail appears the gypsies run. And that is why the gypsies are always on the move, and why Jesus was crucified with only three nails.

Three nails, and three nails only, are always shown among the emblems of the Crucifixion, and the feet of Christ on the cross are shown as transfixed with a single nail. A story is current in the Near East, however, that a gypsy stole the fourth nail from the Cross. Another story to account for the missing fourth nail is that the Roman soldiers used it to stab the smith who made them.

Yet another story connecting the gypsies with the Crucifixion relates that the Virgin Mary cursed the gypsy smith because

he forged the *five* nails for it, and this version is enshrined in a
popular song of the Passion current among the Greek people.

And by a gypsy smith they passed, a smith who nails was making,
"Thou dog, thou gypsy dog," said she, "what is it thou art making?"
"They're going to crucify a man and I the nails am making,
They only ordered three of me, but five I mean to make them,
Two for his knees I design, two for his hands I fashion,
The fifth, the sharpest of the five, within his heart shall enter."

According to legend, God handed out letters to all the races
of mankind, except the gypsies, because they forged the nails
for the Crucifixion.

Another tradition, quoted by A. Long in *The Folklore
Calendar*, states that the gypsies are descended from Samer,
the goldsmith who made the Golden Calf, worshipped by the
Israelites, and who, as a punishment, was turned out of the
tribe, and have been wanderers ever since. There is, of course,
no real evidence that the gypsies were so far west at either
period, though Bercovici writes:

> "I did not go so far as to claim, with Bataillard, that
> they were the ones who brought bronze to Europe. I do
> believe that they brought the art of iron-forging, the dance
> of the East, and orchestral music to the shores of the Black
> Sea, to the Pont Euxine, when they first set foot on
> European soil,"

and seeks to identify them with the Sygynes, the people
beloved of Vulcan because of their skill at the forge, mentioned
by Homer and known to Alexander the Great.

Actually, they would seem to have appeared in Eastern
Europe during the early Middle Ages. Ladislaus of Hungary, in
A.D. 1092, was legislating against "Ishmaelites", who were
possibly gypsies, as they were wandering merchants and blacksmiths. They are considered to have reached various parts of
Western Europe during the fifteenth century, but Bercovici
maintains that they were already in France in 1388, when
members of the "Tinguery" family held official positions at
Abbeville, including one who was the corporation blacksmith.

His argument is based on the name, as one of the many corruptions of Zincar, worker in tin—Tzigane, Tingar (Rumania), Tshingian (Greece), Zincar (Macedonia), Zingari (Italy), Czigany (Hungary), Tinker in Scotland, where they have been much in evidence and even have a "capital", in the village of Yetholm, near the border, and Dengelder, coppersmiths in Germany.

Persecuted, expelled, "liquidated", abused, suspected, hustled, despised, feared, the gypsies, like the Jews, have survived it all, though, with no religion to hold them together, the purity of their blood is not so complete, especially in this country, where the majority are, at best, half-breeds. Always in the past, and often in the present, they have been suspected of sorcery, magic and witchcraft—but so were the early smiths of all primitive races and times. They have never taken to agriculture, which involved a settled life, but, unlike the Jews, they are rarely town-dwellers. Sometimes basket weavers, often horsedealers, musicians as a side-line and by nature, fortune-tellers on the feminine side, they have always been, first and foremost, metal workers, and their skill at smithcraft has sometimes been their salvation, as in France in the seventeenth century, though at the beginning of the fourteenth century the Gitanos of Spain were forbidden to practise the trade of blacksmith, "the one trade in which the gypsies were and are of all peoples the most skilled", and in 1619 Philip III ordered them to settle in cities and towns and forbade them to work as blacksmiths, under pain of death.[1]

But in Borrow's day, besides trafficking in horses and mules and acting as highwaymen, the gypsies of Spain were, and had been for some time, practising the blacksmith's craft. Members of gypsy bands, Borrow says, were allotted the most suitable tasks, so, as with the lame smiths of classic tradition, wielding the hammer and tongs was abandoned to those who, while possessed of athletic forms, were for some physical reason or other unfit for being jockeys or highwaymen.

Their forges were generally in the heart of some mountain or woodland area, where the smith himself felled trees and made his charcoal.

---

[1] *The Story of the Gypsies* (Bercovici).

"Gypsy crafts are strikingly familiar in all parts of the globe—in no part are they agriculturalists or in regular service. We have found them hammering iron and manufacturing from it instruments either for their own use or that of the neighbouring towns and villages. They may be seen employed in a similar manner in the plains of Russia."[1]

In the Basque country, though the gypsies of the village of Cibour are fishermen, they have never totally abandoned their old trade, and the finest kettles of the area come from there. To quote Borrow again:

"A common occupation of the Gitanos of Granada is working in iron, and it is not infrequent to find these caves tenanted by Gypsy smiths and their families, who ply the hammer and forge in the bowels of the earth. To one standing at the mouth of the cave, especially at night, they afford a picturesque spectacle. Gathered round the forge, their bronzed and naked bodies, illuminated by the flame, appear like figures of demons; while the cave, with its flinty sides and uneven roof, blackened by the charcoal vapours which hover about it in festoons, seems to offer no inadequate representation of fabled purgatory."[2]

Rather does it echo the legends of Vulcan most strongly, and suggest how those legends arose.

In the Balkans and the south-east of Europe generally, Greece, Turkey, Macedonia, Jugo-Slavia, Bulgaria, Rumania and Hungary, the gypsies are *the* smiths; "wherever you hear hammer upon anvil, you are certain to find a prato (brother)".[3] The Laeshi of Rumania, darkest and perhaps purest of gypsies, will not mix with others; each of them is a skilled mason, carpenter, blacksmith or mechanic, but they work only long enough to supply their immediate wants. They can pick any lock, duplicate any key, mix metals, repair copper vessels, forge steel and iron, even make needles, with the most primitive tools, and with the same tools they make earrings, rings, bracelets, etc., to sell to the peasants. A hammer, a pair of tongs, a

[1] *The Zincali* (Borrow).
[2] Ibid.
[3] Ibid.

file and a small home-made bellows are carried on the back of
every member of the tribe and the same tools are used for any
work they do. They despise the gypsy musicians who sing and
play at non-gypsy festivals.[1] Of fourteen trade corporations of
the Laeshi, or Laetzi, five are metal-working crafts—the Cal-
derarii, tinkers, the Ferarii, ironsmiths, the Castarii, coppersmiths, the Potcavarii, blacksmiths, the Mesterilacatachi,
ironsmiths selling keys and bars of iron, while a sixth section
are sorcerers and fortune-tellers.[2]

In Hungary, the Caldereros are coppersmiths; in Italy, the
Zingari are cattle dealers and iron forgers, as well as masons.
The gypsy coppersmiths of Hungary and the Balkans work on
prehistoric lines, in front of their tents. They make a hole in
the ground, and in this they light the charcoal used. At one
end of the hole they fix a funnel with one terminal in the fire,
and the bellows at the other. A boy works the bellows, and at
five years of age is an expert.[3] Some forty years ago a band
of such coppersmiths made a sudden appearance in England,
but did not remain; Mr. Fred Shaw, a friend of the present
author, and a man whose character and erudition should have
earned him a better knowledge by his countrymen, visited and
photographed them, but he would never publish his photo-
graphs, since, he maintained, he procured them by gaining the
Romany confidence, which he would not betray. He was, it
may be mentioned, a fluent speaker of the Romany language.

So much are the gypsies of Eastern Europe wedded to the
forge that the people round about Viganj (Jugo-Slavia) were
known as Firaurio Pharaohs, Egyptian ironworkers, and their
three villages are Vigany (bellows), Nadkovan (anvil) and
Kovacevici (smiths).[4] In Scandinavia, despite the Norse forge
tradition, they are coppersmiths, iron forgers and blacksmiths,
as well as cattle dealers, and these occupations have been so
much identified in recent times with the gypsies that, in the
popular language, anyone working at them has been called
Tzigani or Heiden (pagan), even if he was not a gypsy.[5]

In these islands, save for occasional inruptions from the

[1] *The Story of the Gypsies* (Bercovici).
[2] *Rumanian Journey* (Sacheverell Sitwell).
[3] *Raggle-Taggle* (Starkie).
[4] *A Wayfarer in Jugo-Slavia* (L. F. Edwards).
[5] *The Story of the Gypsies* (Bercovici).

Continent, the smithy does not play a prominent part in gypsy life at the present time, though the strong Smith clan of gypsies in East Anglia suggests a past connection with the forge. Their metal working here is mostly with the gypsy tinkers, and even these are more evident in Scotland than in England; Scottish gypsies, too, live far nearer the original gypsy mode than the majority of gypsies or half-gypsies south of the border, despite the settled habits of the gypsy border stronghold, Yetholm. In the New Forest they are flower-sellers, clothes-peg makers and the like—with never a smith among them, despite the old charcoal industry of the Forest.

CHAPTER XV

THE SONG OF THE ANVIL

As great Pythagoras of yore,
Standing beside the blacksmith's door,
And hearing the hammers, as they smote
The anvils with a different note,
Stole from the varying tones that hung
Vibrant on every iron tongue,
The secret of the sounding wire,
And formed the seven-chorded lyre.

LONGFELLOW: To a Child.

As the weaver plied the shuttle, wove he too the mystic rhyme,
And the smith his iron measures hammered to the anvil's chime,
Thanking God, whose boundless wisdom makes the flowers of
      poesy bloom,
In the forge's dust and cinders, in the tissues of the loom.

LONGFELLOW: Nuremburg.

"By Artevelde! what are drums, cymbals, fifes, viols and bag-
pipes worth? For heavenly music give me my sledges beating, my
anvils ringing, my bellows roaring, my good workmen singing and
hammering."

Legend of Smetse Smee. (CHARLES DE COSTER:
Flemish Legends.)

IT IS strange that, with the twang of the bow suggesting the
stringed instruments, the draught through the reed or hollow
bamboo starting the family of wood instruments, and the
hollow tree-trunk or the stretched hide forming the ancestry
of the drum, there is no orchestral instrument the origin of
which can definitely be attributed to the sound of the hammer
on the anvil. The nearest approaches are the triangle, the
xylophone and the bells; the triangle, however, is descended
from the systrum of the Egyptian priests, which has no apparent
connection with the smithy, and the xylophone is too modern
to be attributed to such a source by descent, though it might

be the outcome of subconscious suggestion. The music of the
bells, though, has a distinct connection with the forge. The
earliest great bells were made of wrought-iron plates laid over
one another and riveted together—the work of the blacksmith
—and there can be little doubt that the whole idea of bell
music was suggested by the sound of hammer upon anvil: early
bells were, indeed, rung with a hammer. The bellows of the
organ, too, introduced into Western European music about
the eighth century A.D., seems obviously to have been taken
from the bellows of the forge.

Apart from all this mechanical connection, there is, from
the outset, a strong association between music, poesy and
the forge. Agni, Aryan god of fire, was the source of poetic
inspiration; Brigit, Celtic goddess of fire, was goddess of
poetry and patroness of the smiths; Lugh, Celtic sun-god, was
a smith, harpist, poet and taleteller. There is a chain of
analogy connecting smithcraft and the forge with the softer
arts which the ancients were not slow to observe. They were
virtually of one accord in seeing the parallel between poetic
fire and the actual thing; the forge was a daughter of the hearth
and the hearth the nurse of the poetic muse. At a very early
stage, too, man possessed a sense of rhythm—it was present in
most of his elementary activities, industrial or recreative, and
he and his feminine companions played ball rhythmically,
developing time and rhythm with the hands and feet. He could
not fail to notice the rhythm in nature; Pythagoras was at the
root of things in his vision of the harmony of the spheres. In
the work of the forge, rhythm was not merely natural, it was a
necessity.[1] Borrow was echoing a distant past in his dictum
that there is something poetical about a forge; Hesiod had
discovered that two and a half millennia before, since he was
woodman, agriculturalist, blacksmith, maker of ploughs, and
poet.[2]

Regin, the smith-tutor of Sigurd, in Norse mythology,
"beardless and low of stature, of visage pinched and wan",

---

[1] In the Goldsmiths' Pageant of St. Dunstan, in London, there were
"workmen at work, keeping excellent time in their strokes upon the anvil".
[2] It occurs to me that the ploughs Hesiod made may have been entirely of
wood, but Gompertz, in *The Master Craftsmen*, describes him as a smith.
F. W. R.

was deft in every cunning, save the dealing of the sword;
So sweet was his tongue-speech fashioned, that men trowed his
                                                    every word;
His hand with the harp strings blended was the mingle of delight
With the latter days of sorrow; all tales he told aright.
The Master of the Masters in the smithying craft was he.

Under his tuition, Sigurd mastered the smith's craft and the
art of carving runes; he learned languages, music and eloquence,
as well as being a warrior-hero.[1] The Teutonic sword, the master-
piece of the Teutonic smith, was invested with magic power
through spells and runes; Sir Walter Scott suggests that the
spell was *sung*—for "Thorbiorn, the Danish armourer, spoke of
a spell he had for making breastplates, by singing a certain
song while the iron was heating," he makes Henry Gow say,
in *The Fair Maid of Perth.* It is not unlikely. Borrow speaks
of making his horseshoe to the tune of a gypsy song, timing
his operations by it, just as rural housewives have timed their
cooking to hymns! It only needed a wondering rustic or
ignorant fighter to watch a wonderful craftsman at his awe-
striking work, singing while he did it, for an assumption to
grow that there was a connection between song and task, as
indeed there was if the rhythm of the task was in the song.
    Scott makes his hero-smith of *The Fair Maid of Perth* a
poet and a fiddler, "though the blast of the bellows and the
clatter of the anvil make but coarse company to lays of min-
strelsy". Wherein he was wrong, like Pythagoras when he laid
it down that the music of the spheres was unheard because we
are like men in a smithy forge, who cease to be aware of the
sound which they constantly hear and are never in a position
to contrast it with silence. There is a palpable rhythm even in
machinery, and the smith's work is not so monotonously con-
tinuous as to benumb the senses. It is interesting to note,
incidentally, that, apart from Scott's delineation of Henry Gow,
two notable members of the Gows, the smith clan, were Neil
Gow, "the prince of Scottish fiddlers and composer of many
popular reels" (1727–1807), and his son Nathaniel (1766–1831).
    Among primitive peoples, the association of smith and
musician is closer, more regular and more apparent. In India,

[1] *Myths of the Norsemen* (Guerber).

the Kotas, a very low caste, are musicians, gold and silver smiths. Among the Hunzas, the Bericho, who have some gypsy affinities, are not only the blacksmiths, but are also musicians with drums and pipes.[1] The blacksmiths of the Tuaregs of the Sahara also act as heralds and bards. Unlike the position among the Celtic races, where the smith was honoured—and often bracketed with the bard or musician—the smith-musician is despised among the eastern nations, and it is interesting to note that the status is high or low in both cases alike: the smith is raised or depressed with the musician.

With the Lambas of Northern Rhodesia, though the performance of music in itself is not the prerogative of the smith, the makers of certain special instruments held in high esteem throughout the race are smiths of particular skill.

It is, however, among the gypsy folk that the association is strongest. The Kauliyah of Irak, reputedly gypsies, are black-smiths and fiddlers, dancers and singers.

> "Whatever gypsies do or whatever they are, there is some instrument of music in their hands, and they are almost always engaged in producing music, melodies, accompaniments, dance and mirth," says Bercovici,[2]

and, in another passage:

> "There is no music but gypsy music in Rumania; even the songs of the peasants are gypsy songs. All melodic life, not only of the Rumanians, but of all the peoples of the Balkan peninsula, and probably beyond its borders, is of gypsy origin."

Even more or less sedentary gypsies in the large towns, often half-breeds, are mostly musicians; the town of Braila had the largest gypsy quarter in Rumania and furnished the greatest number of musicians, the usual instruments of the Tziganes being the violin, the cobza (resembling a mandolin), mascalur and cembalo (a primitive portable piano played on open strings with two curved sticks).[3] In South Serbia, all the smiths are

---

[1] *Language Hunting in the Karakoram* (E. O. Lorimer).
[2] *The Story of the Gypsies* (Konrad Bercovici—a Rumanian).
[3] Ibid.

I

gypsies as well as the professional musicians. In Hungary, the gypsies are master-craftsmen and musicians. Only in Russia and the Basque country are the gypsies unmusical, but in the latter area they are great dancers.

"Gypsy musicians sprang from the forge," writes Professor Starkie of the Spanish gypsies.[1] The martinetes are songs of the forge, and "the only accompaniment worthy of the martinete was the clang of the hammer on the anvil". Opera lovers will not need to be reminded of the effectiveness and appropriateness of the anvil accompaniment to the gypsy chorus in *Il Trovatore*. Longfellow, in his *Spanish Student*, too, opens Scene V with gypsies at the forge, singing. In the poesy of smithing, "Las muchis" ("the sparks") is eloquent: "More than a hundred lovely daughters I see produced at one time, fiery as roses, in one moment they expire gracefully, circumvolving"—a metaphor which appears among both the Spaniards and the gypsies.[2]

A century or so ago, there were excellent musicians among the gypsies of the New Forest, especially violinists, but things are different now, and the New Forest gypsies are not smiths. In Finland, smithing is hereditary among the gypsies, and a son of the forge may be the accordion or other player at the village dance.[3]

And we mere gorgios? Well, many of us can still tune our ears with pleasure to the ring of hammer on anvil in the quiet of a rustic village as well as to the bells in the calm of the evening—first cousins in the unspoilt countryside.

At Sturminster Newton, in Dorset, the band of bellringers includes two smiths, father and son, and Baring Gould wrote of father and son in Cornwall who were "smiths and bards".

[1] *Don Gypsy* (Starkie).
[2] *The Zincali* (Borrow).
[3] "Finnish Solstice" (Miss B. H. Wright, in the *Geographical Magazine*, May, 1939).

CHAPTER XVI

GRETNA GREEN

"Ay, ay," said the postillion, "till the old people are
pacified and they send you letters directed to the next
post town, to be left until called for, beginning with 'Dear
children', and enclosing you each a cheque for one hundred
pounds, when you will leave this place and go home in a
coach like gentlefolks, to visit your governors."

.   .   .   .   .

"Just come from Gretna Green, and already quarrel-
ing," said the postillion.
"We do not come from Gretna Green," said Belle.
"Ah, I had forgot," said the postillion, "none but great
people go to Gretna Green."
GEORGE BORROW: *Lavengro.*

THE fire and the hearth have been associated with marriage
and its rites from the earliest times. Agni, Hindu god of fire,
was god of marriage too. The Hindu marriage rite, like many
others, involved ceremonies around the domestic fire or a
special fire; Greek marriages culminated in the lighting of the
new fire from the parental hearths. The basis of these ceremonies, however, was more the sanctity and the family associations of the domestic hearth than necessarily the divinity of
the fire itself, though in some cases this enters into the matter
also, consciously or subconsciously.

There is a closer association with the smith and the forge in
the old Norse ceremony in which the wedding tie was supposed
to be consecrated by Thor's hammer. Brides wore red, Thor's
favourite colour, and still a favourite colour with the womenfolk of Norway, and for the same reason rings in the older north
were almost always set with a red stone. The ring itself, it must
be remembered, was originally a product of the smith, and, in
the north of Europe it was one of his main products. Originally
the ring was a mark of honour or reward among Norsemen, not
specially associated with matrimony; the use of the ring as
a wedding pledge followed the earlier custom of an interchange
of presents.

Christina Hole, in *English Folklore*, suggests that the "sacred character of smiths" is attested by marriages in the smithy. That sacred character, which is severely localized in its incidence, however, is attached not so much to the smith himself as to the divine element of fire in the first instance, and secondarily to the magic properties of the metal with which his wonders are worked. If the smith himself is credited with supernatural powers, they are more the powers of the wizard and the sorcerer than those of the priest or the divine representative.

The informal marriages for which Gretna Green and its smithy are famous were simply the result of the lax marriage laws of Scotland, and the fact that Gretna Green was an easily accessible village just across the border. There was no special virtue in a marriage in the smithy: any reputable witness would do. Possibly the old reverence paid to the forge invested Gretna Green's smithy marriages with more prominence or significance than the many similar informal unions effected at the Scottish border in which neither smith nor smithy are concerned. Possibly some special potency may have been attached to the ceremony in the smithy because of those old traditions. Tradition is often subconscious rather than conscious in its influence, and it is often strong in the very quarters which profess to be free from it, or even deride it! Or, there may have been a fashionable craze for the smithy. Illogical fashions in weddings and their settings are not unknown today, especially in ultra-modern countries.

The fact remains, historically, that Gretna Green was not the only village just across the Scoto-English border at which marriages were celebrated without the aid of priest or official and that, in Gretna Green itself, such marriages took place just as often at the toll-house, the ferry, or elsewhere, as at the smithy—perhaps even more often at the toll-house. And, finally, alas for the sacred fire—the smith marriages seem to have taken place across the anvil, not at the forge. But the Gretna Green blacksmith *did* tie the knot often enough, even if he was not alone in doing so—so Gretna Green must figure, even if cursorily, in the annals of the forge. The custom was abolished by law in 1940, but in January, 1952, a twenty-three-year-old American soldier and a German girl arrived to be married over the anvil—twelve years too late!

CHAPTER XVII

THE SMITH-ARTIST

"By hammer in hand
All arts do stand."

> (Inscription over a smithy at New
> Abbey, near Dumfries, and on the
> banner of the Smiths', Cutlers' and
> Plumbers' Company in the Gros-
> venor Museum, Chester.)

ON THE Continent, the German handicraft guilds, which had
obtained recognition in the fourteenth century, were still
regulating their trades long after the Middle Ages. There were
the city guilds, of specialist character, and rural guilds, cover-
ing wheelwrights, cobblers, tailors, joiners, potters, smiths and
the like. Some of the city guilds were exclusive in their member-
ship and specialist in their qualifications; in Nuremberg, particularly, there were awl-smiths, coppersmiths, bellfounders,
gold and silver wiredrawers, etc. Trades, too, were distinguished
as coarse or fine; in the former were counted the ordinary
smiths, in the latter were spur, file and lock smiths. With the
generality of the guilds, as soon as an apprentice finished his
term, he, for three or four years, travelled from place to place,
working as an itinerant journeyman.

Every handicraft had its herberge, or inn, in a town; there
the travelling "gesell", or journeyman, resorted on his arrival
in the place, finding there his home until he could procure work
or proceeded on his journey, and to it the masters came when
wanting hands. The herberge was also the meeting-place of
the guild; from the ceiling depended the insignia of the trade
to which it belonged: in the case of the smiths a horseshoe,
adorned with coloured ribbons. A village herberge, however,
might be common to all the handicrafts and the insignia of the

133

various trades would be suspended over the different tables
where the members of the different handicraft ssat. Apprentice-
ships varied from three to six years, followed by the years
of wandering. At the end of the apprenticeship period, the
apprentice was declared free and provided with a Wander
Book, containing testimony to that effect, as well as his
birth and apprenticeship certificates. Then, with knapsack
on his back and stick in hand, he set out on his long
pilgrimage.

If, in a given town, there was no work to be had, the local
guild would make the traveller a pecuniary grant, on condition
that he proceeded on his way without more than a day's delay.
A gesell could receive no monetary assistance if he had refused
work offered to him, had been in the place within the previous
three months and received either work or a contribution, or
was not provided with the proper certificates. When the gesell
received work, he had to deliver up his Wander Book, to be kept
in the guild chest until his departure. If master and man
wished to discontinue the employment, eight days' notice was
necessary, and the man working "by the piece" must complete
his piece of work before leaving; if otherwise, employment
must terminate on a Saturday evening. If dismissed, the man
could take work in the same place, but if he himself gave
the notice he must absent himself from the town for at
least fourteen days before taking other employment in it. Mis-
conduct involved being put on the black list and reported to
the police.[1]

This system of itineracy survived until well on in the nineteenth century, and gave the young craftsman an experience
and knowledge of what was being done elsewhere which the
man working all his life in one place could hardly acquire,
whatever its disadvantages otherwise may have been. At the
conclusion of the wandering period, if the journeyman wanted
to become a master, he had to produce his "master-piece" for
the judgment of the masters in the guild.

Such a system, no doubt, had much to do with the growth
of ornamental ironworking on the Continent during the
Renaissance, together with the fact that grilles, wellheads and
the like gave to the Continental smith more scope than the

[1] *Rural Life in Germany* (William Howitt, 1842).

rural craftsman of England had. Famous names arose among the Continental craftsmen in iron, such as Quentin Matsys, responsible for the superstructure of the great well by Antwerp cathedral, the ironwork of which is an outstanding specimen of the art of the smith,[1] and George Heuss of Nuremberg, who made the iron railings round the shrine of St. Sebald, the clock-work of the Frauenkirke, and the mechanism for drawing water at the deep well on the Paniersburg. Nuremberg, too, produced Hans Grunavalt, who died in 1503, and his son-in-law, Wilhelm von Worms, famous armourers both.

In Scandinavia, an increased demand for ironwork in the sixteenth century led to a revival of craftsmanship, and certain districts became famous for particular products—Dalarna for scythes, Vastergotland for knives, Närke for spikes. Later, towards the close of the seventeenth century, the peasant smiths had become prosperous and artistically ambitious, turning out pendants in the form of leaves, foliated crosses and elaborate lighting appliances. Magnificent candlesticks and coronæ were turned out on the anvil, with twisted work, drops, and hammered cockerels—the symbol of light.

English craftsmen, unequalled in their work in good quality wrought-iron products of useful purpose and simple elegance, were slow to follow the new fashion of ornament and elabora-tion. Late in the seventeenth century, however, Jean Tijou, a Huguenot refugee, who arrived from Holland with William of Orange in 1689, led the renascence of English ornamental iron-working, turning out railings, gates, panels, pilasters, for mansions and for St. Paul's Cathedral; such work was still not quite divorced from ordinary smithing, for, according to Mr. Starkie Gardner, Tijou's first work at St. Paul's consisted of the iron frames for the large ground-floor windows, charged at 6d. per pound, equal to about £48 each, exclusive of two vertical iron stays filled in with alternate circles and lozenges, charged as "grotesque". Tijou produced the whole of the lower tier of windows and all above those in the choir, transepts and west front, his deliveries of such ironwork extending from 1691 to 1697.[2] It is said that he was more a designer than a working

---

[1] Described in the author's *Story of Water Supply*.
[2] *Ironwork* (Starkie Gardner), quoted in Briggs' *Short History of the Building Crafts*.

smith, and, like the celebrated furniture-makers of the eighteenth century, he published his designs in book form; hereditary
traditions, custom and individual ingenuity were being assailed,
in all crafts, by the copyist, heralding the mass producer of
modern days.

During the closing years of the seventeenth century, and
through the eighteenth, many of the English blacksmiths took
up decorative ironwork. Not many have left their names behind
them, despite the fact that a large number could, and did, turn
out work of architectural value. A few, like Robert Bakewell of
Derbyshire, and William Edney of Bristol, who made some
very beautiful gates for the church of St. Mary Redclyffe[1] in
that city, in 1710, turned their whole attention to the production of elegant wrought-iron gates, stairways and balconies,
for churches, town houses and country mansions. Sometimes a
whole family of smiths became notable for their artistic work,
as in the case of the Davies family of Y Groes Foel, Bersham,
near Wrexham. The father, Hugh Davies, who died in 1702,
is reputed to have made the fine choir rail of Wrexham
church and a fine gate to Malpas churchyard, in Cheshire.
He left four sons and six daughters. At least two, or three,
of the sons were skilled smiths, and tradition has it that one
of the daughters was, too! Robert and John were the outstanding craftsmen of the family, and have left their work
in Cheshire, Flintshire, Montgomeryshire, Denbighshire and
Shropshire.[2]

A similar process was at work, though, in ironwork, as had
taken place rather earlier in stonework. To a large extent, in
the Middle Ages, the master-mason was his own architect: it
was not until the sixteenth century that the professional
architect began to take designing out of his hands. So also, in
the eighteenth century, the architect took to designing ornamental ironwork, and the furniture designer to drawing
grates, leaving the smith, in the main, only to carry out their
ideas.

During the Victorian era the elegance of wrought iron all
too often gave place to the extensive use of ugly, harsh castings,

[1] Originally across the chancel, but now under the tower.
[2] Dr. Iorwerth Peate, in the Guide to the Collection of Welsh Crafts and
Industries, National Museum of Wales.

used not only where wrought-iron work might have been more artistically and equally usefully employed, but also in many places where iron itself was entirely out of place. Most of the cast-iron pillars, columns, balconies, and the like, have had a very short life in terms of architectural survival, and there is now a definite revival in the use of elegant wrought-iron designs, for lighting brackets, gates, railings and other such purposes.

A good deal of this work is done by specialist smiths, working on little else, and in urban workshops, but there are still some village smiths who are artists in wrought iron, and the Rural Industries Bureau has done good work in encouraging others to take it up, introducing new equipment to them, and advising them. The main difficulty is to enlist the younger generation, most of whom prefer to flock to the towns, with their cinemas and other amenities, and few of whom are interested in craftsmanship. Smith training schools have been instituted in some parts, and the Worshipful Company of Blacksmiths award a medal for the most distinctive work in Britain.

There is art, though, in the simplest smith work. To quote the author of *English Country Crafts* (Norman Wymer):

"A man who can heat solid bars of iron and then hammer them into whatever shapes he likes, and weld, rivet or bolt them together into models of such artistic perfection, relying almost entirely on his eye for measurements, can surely have no superiors in craftsmanship. It is his very skill in fire-welding together two pieces of iron that distinguishes good from indifferent work, and which is the key to the uniqueness of his craft. He must bring his iron to the highest temperature it will stand without burning or dis-integrating, and yet be sure that it is hot enough for him to fuse the two pieces into one. A fraction of a second's delay in whipping them out of the fire and hammer-ing them together on the anvil means the failure of a weld."

The present author, who has had some experience of

welding with oxy-acetylene, in another connection, has always maintained that good welders are born rather than made, and, since the hereditary element has always been and still is to a large extent a feature of the blacksmithing fraternity, this probabl applies equally to forge welding and all other phases of the smith's work.

An eighteenth-century
blacksmith's sign

CHAPTER XVIII

THE SMITH'S FUEL

The little widow of good Count Laurel
Has no one left her for kiss or quarrel,
I want a sweetheart and find me none,
Charcoal woman must live alone.

(*Chorus*) Who would say that the charcoal woman
Sooty, sooty charcoal woman,
In all the city and all the land,
Could find a lover to kiss her hand.

(Spanish children's song, quoted by Bates
in *Highways and Byways in Spain*.)

BUT charcoal has been wedded to the forge for many centuries!
Charcoal, as a fuel, is astonishingly ancient and widespread in
its use, ranging as it does all over the world from the extreme
east to the extreme west and southwards through Africa, and
from the dim recesses of the untold past until the present day.
It has been markedly the fuel of the smith until recent times;
sometimes he provided his own, sometimes he procured it
from professional charcoal burners, and sometimes his client
had to provide it. The Chinese travelling brazier or tinker
carries all he needs with him save for a few sticks of charcoal,
and these he procures from the household whose work he is
going to do.

Though some woods are better for charcoal making than
others, much of course has to depend on the timber available in
the locality, and an astonishing variety has been used in ancient
times. An Iron Age settlement at Meon Hill, Hampshire,
yielded charcoal made from oak, maple, sycamore, hawthorn,
hazel, plum or cherry, ash, elm, willow, poplar, apple or pear,
lime and blackthorn—but mostly the first seven of these. Charcoal found in the Roman remains at Caerleon was made from
hazel, hawthorn, willow, oak, and a variety of prunus which
has been identified as either cherry or blackthorn, probably the
latter, with oak as by far the most common material. It will be

seen that this selection was virtually the same as the first seven varieties in the Iron Age list. Mr. F. Mansell, in *The Wayfarer's Book*, gives "alder for oast houses, oak and ash for the steel industry, lime for artists' pencils, birch and chestnut for chemical charcoal", and quotes:

> Jove's oak, the warlike ash, vein'd elm, the softer birch,
> Short hazel, maple plain, light ash, the bending wych,
> Tough holly and smooth beech, may all together burn.

In Spain, laurel was used for making charcoal.

In much of the Orient and round about the Mediterranean, charcoal is a general purpose fuel, often the only fuel in settled communities; in other parts it is the fuel of the metal worker.

In many parts, charcoal making is a regular trade, yielding sufficient fuel not only for local requirements but for outside sale as well. In *The Valleys of the Assassins*, Miss Freya Stark refers to a regular traffic in charcoal across Luristan (Persia), the charcoal, she says, taking three days to make—which seems short—and the journey with it to Nihavend four days, making seven days' work, for which the charcoal burners receive the equivalent of 2s. 5d. In parts of the East, especially in China, the wholesale tree-cutting involved has led to serious consequences in the timber denudation of the countryside and the desiccation of the soil. So great was the destruction of trees by the Arabs, even the roots being "burned" for charcoal, that, under the Turkish rule, a law was made prohibiting the destruction of trees. Many trees were probably invested with an aura of sanctity purely for their preservation, as cows were in ancient Egypt.

Corsica exports charcoal to France, Spain, Italy and Sardinia: the charcoal burners cut down thick stems of arbutus and other plants and stack around the heap smaller pieces of wood, the whole pile being covered over with green leaves and earth, and a hole being left on one side through which the fire is lighted. The charcoal is ready in about ten days, and it takes nearly an acre of shrubs, about ten tons of brushwood, to produce a ton of charcoal.[1]

In the method and with the woods used in this country, the

---

[1] *Corsica* (E. Young, 1909).

charcoal burner cuts and stores his piles of timber during the winter; about four tons of wood are required for a ton of charcoal, and the different kinds yield different qualities. When the weather begins to improve, the wood is sorted into different thicknesses, to ensure even smouldering, and cut into billets of about three feet in length. A stake is driven into the centre of the clearing, to form the focal point of the "hearth". Three billets are then laid around the centre stake, in triangular formation, with ends overlapping, three more superimposed, and so on until a triangular chimney about three to four feet high results. Then the remaining billets to be used are stood on end with a cant towards the centre, to form a dome about three feet high; the thicker billets are placed nearest the centre of the cone and the thinner on the outside, an air space being left between. Short billets are placed horizontally on the top of the pile, radiating from the chimney like the spokes of a wheel. A dome thus being eventually formed, looking like a native hut about five feet high, it is finally roofed with grass, straw or heather and covered with damp earth. Then the stake is taken out and burning embers dropped down the chimney to start the fire. The hole is filled with unlighted charcoal and sealed with turf.

During the burning process, which takes about a week, the charcoal burner lives in a hut close by, to watch the fire, as the wood must be charred and never burn; water is thrown on the ashes and holes are watched for, as if too much air is admitted the pile would catch fire. As an additional safeguard, the hearth may be sheltered from draughts by hurdles. When the wood is all "burnt", and only black, hard charcoal remains, it is either allowed to cool down or quenched by throwing water on it.

Though a certain amount of peat was mixed with charcoal for the forges in Lancashire, and probably elsewhere where peat was readily available, it was the charcoal available that brought the iron industry to the Wealden areas of Sussex and Kent from the thirteenth century onwards, and the New Forest "exported" the fuel to other parts in the seventeenth century, a large proportion to the mining and smelting areas of Cornwall: charcoal making had been a New Forest occupation for many centuries then, and the name of Purkis, the charcoal burner who found the body of William Rufus, is still to be found there. During the sixteenth century enormous quantities of wood were being turned into charcoal for ironworking, the quantity used by the two Sussex mills at Sheffield and Worth alone being about 2,700,000 cubic feet of timber in less than two years.[1]

In 1580, it was stated that a beech tree of one foot square "at the stubbe" would make one and a half loads of charcoal, and the ironworks at Monkswood, near Tintern, would require six hundred such trees every year. Obviously, if the process had gone on, disastrous results would have accrued, similar to those in unordered regions of the Orient. To prevent this, Acts were passed in 1558, 1581 and 1585 regulating the cutting of wood for furnaces and prohibiting the use of timber trees for charcoal, but the destruction still went on, inevitably so with no real alternative and economical fuel available for forging or smelting, though obviously the smiths and cutlers of Hereford were using "sea-coal"—the name given to mineral coal to distinguish it from charcoal—in Elizabeth's reign, since they then presented a petition against forestallers and regraters, resulting in the general public being forbidden to buy coal until twelve noon. In 1603, George Owen, writing of his county of Pembrokeshire, said, "this countrie groneth with the generalle complaint of other countries of the decreasage of wood", several forests having utterly disappeared. The first successful use of coal for iron smelting is generally credited to Dud Dudley, in 1620, and the development of its use in the following century lessened the use of both charcoal and wood fires.[2] In New England, the virgin forests rendered the problem less urgent and charcoal burning for the ironworks was in full swing there throughout the seventeenth century. Charcoal still remains the regular fuel of the primitive smith in many parts of the world, and its original use on the forge, with the consequent incorporation of carbon with the iron, is considered to have been the cause of the first accidental production of steel.

---

[1] *English Industries of the Middle Ages* (Salzman).
[2] In 1697 Celia Frennes refers to "Sea-coale at Newcastle" as "what the smiths use and it cakes in the fire and makes greate heate".

CHAPTER XIX

THE VILLAGE BLACKSMITH

Under a spreading chestnut tree
The village smithy stands;
The smith, a mighty man is he,
With large and sinewy hands;
And the muscles of his brawny arms
Are strong as iron bands.

His hair is crisp and black and long,
His face is like the tan;
His brow is wet with honest sweat,
He earns whate'er he can
And looks the whole world in the face,
For he owes not any man.

Week in, week out, from morn till night,
You can hear his bellows blow,
You can hear him swing his heavy sledge
With measured beat and slow,
Like a sexton ringing the village bell
When the evening sun is low.

And children coming home from school
Look in at the open door;
They love to see the flaming forge
And hear the bellows roar,
And catch the burning sparks that fly
Like chaff from a threshing-floor.

.   .   .   .   .

Toiling, rejoicing, sorrowing,
Onward through life he goes;
Each morning sees some task begin,
Each evening sees it close;
Something attempted, something done,
Has earned a night's repose.

Thanks, thanks to thee, my worthy friend,
For the lesson thou hast taught!

Thus at the flaming forge of life
Our fortunes must be wrought,
Thus, on its sounding anvils shaped
Each burning deed and thought.

LONGFELLOW.

IF BORROW is the novelist of the forge, assuredly Longfellow is its poet. There are allusions in many of his other poems to it, and in his long poem, *Evangeline*, the hero of the story is a blacksmith's son, a fact which gives him the opportunity for another descriptive passage:

Gabriel Lajeunesse, the son of Basil the blacksmith,
Who was a mighty man in the village, and honoured of all men,
For, since the birth of time, throughout all ages and nations,
Has the craft of the smith been held in repute by the people.

. . . . .

Swiftly they hurried away to the forge of Basil the blacksmith,
There at the door they stood, with wondering eyes to behold him,
Take in his leathern lap the hoof of the horse as a plaything,
Nailing the shoe in its place; while near him the tire of the cartwheel,
Lay like a fiery snake, coiled round in a circle of cinders.
Oft on autumnal eves, when without in the gathering darkness
Bursting with light seemed the smithy, through every cranny and
crevice,
Warm by the forge within, they watched the labouring bellows,
And, as its panting ceased and the sparks expired in the ashes,
Merrily laughed and said they were nuns going into the chapel.

A telling and vivid description of an English village smithy that—and yet its pattern was not drawn from Old but New England. Both *The Village Blacksmith* itself and Longfellow's obviously ever-present picture of the rural forge are drawn from a village smithy near his home at Cambridge, Massachusetts.[1] On the poet's seventy-second birthday, in 1879, the children of Cambridge presented him with a chair made from the wood of the blacksmith's chestnut tree, and the old man thereupon wrote a poem, a copy of which he gave to every

[1] The home of the smith, Dexter Pratt, still stands, but is now a restaurant and shop.

child who visited him and sat in the chair. The picture of the forge was still with him and inspired the verses:

> There, by the blacksmith's forge, beside the street,
> Its blossoms white and sweet
> Enticed the bees until it seemed alive
> And murmured like a hive.

> .　　　.　　　.　　　.　　　.

> I see the smithy, with its fires aglow,
> I hear the bellows blow,
> And the shrill hammers on the anvil beat
> The iron white with heat.

If the source of the inspiration had not been known, there are smithies in England to which the credit might have been given. The village of Milton Abbas in Dorset, transplanted from its original site in the eighteenth century, has chestnut trees planted down its village street, and one is hard by the smithy, which, however, lacks the rustic charm of a less "artistic" structure. The present author remembers a smithy which once stood on the main road into Bournemouth, in its older suburb of Pokesdown (Puck's Down—once a heathland dotted with prehistoric barrows): this had a chestnut tree close to it. Both smithy and chestnut tree disappeared some years ago, obliterated by the growing urbanism and the necessity for enlarging the local railway station. Only in 1953, the smith at Wymeswald, Leicestershire, abandoned his four-hundred-year-old smithy, with chestnut tree, for a new smithy of his own design.

During the nineteenth century the blacksmith still remained an important local craftsman, despite the increasing concentration of ironworking in the engineering works and iron foundries. Even in the engineering city of Lincoln, there were eight blacksmiths plying their trade in 1856 (*English Town Crafts*, N. Wymer). If he did not make as much, the smith repaired more, but perhaps he became more and more the farrier. In these days, even horseshoes are sometimes bought ready made, though most country smiths make their own.

Weapons of war had long since ceased to claim the workmanship of the local smith in Europe. It was not so in the wilder parts of the world; in 1866, when the French were fighting the

K

Koreans, every scrap of iron was collected by the latter, and the forges of the blacksmiths were busy day and night making arms and even turning farmers' tools into pikes and sabres, just as the village smiths must have done for the ill-fated followers of Monmouth in the seventeenth century.

Professor George Trevelyan, in his *English Social History*, suggests that, by the end of Victoria's reign in our country, the village blacksmith was, in some places, the only craftsman left, eking out a declining business in horseshoes by mending the punctured bicycle tyres of tourists. The last part of this dictum is possibly more picturesque than strictly accurate. Bicycle repairs do not seem to have brought more than a little extra to the smithy, though it was a Dumfriesshire blacksmith, Kirkpatrick Macmillan, who is said to have invented the bicycle; at any rate, he is definitely credited with having applied pedals with connecting rods, working on the rear axle, to the tricycle, in 1834.

John Williams of Tremadog, too, smith *and bard*, invented a velocipede in 1856, parts of which, with others of his inventions, are in the National Museum of Wales.[1] The smith has

always had to be a versatile and adaptable craftsman. Often he is the only metal worker for miles around, and sometimes he is wheelwright too. With the decline in farriery,[2] some smithies, like many local agricultural engineering works, have been turned

Bicycle made by T. & H. King, blacksmiths, Wimborne, Dorset, 1872

[1] The Poole Museum possesses a bicycle, with solid forks and cork pedals, made by T. & H. King, Wimborne blacksmiths, in 1872, and a tricycle made by King and Curtis in 1873 for the Wimborne postman.

[2] In 1939 there were 845,854 horses in England and Wales, 548,921 of them on agricultural work; in 1945, 678,653 and 456,840 respectively (*Crafts of the Countryside* (E. J. Stowe)), and the process is still, of course, going on.

into garages, but others have taken on side-lines, such as grinding lawn-mowers. E. J. Stowe, in *Crafts of the Countryside*, writes of one smith who had become the village barber, and cut hair beside the forge, and of two in Yorkshire who ran riding schools. Often the smithy adds to its revenue by being a bill-posting station. Where there are other village handicrafts a smith may make the tools for the village craftsmen. In sheep-farming areas, the smith makes shepherds' crooks, in them-selves an interesting study in local fashions. In Wiltshire, a few smiths echo the early Middle Ages by making bells, though for sheep, not for churches. Originally these sheep bells, varying in size and tone, were, like the early church bells, made of thin iron, riveted together, and a former smith of Great Cheverell, Bill Lancaster, was so renowned for his bells that shepherds would say they could easily distinguish a "Cheverell" bell.[1]

A Dorset village, Iwerne Minster, was renowned, not so long ago, for its wrought-iron signs turned out by the village smithy; the smith's own sign of hammer and tongs still remains at a smithy no longer in use. Here, too, John Brine, blacksmith and locksmith, one of a long line in the craft, made the clock at the village church, using part of a gate and agricultural implements, as well as the clock at the neighbouring village at Fontmell Magna. Both were provided with mechanism for playing hymn tunes. It is interesting to note that two tradesmen of Horsham, Sussex, were still called "clocksmiths" early in the nineteenth century.

In the nineteenth century, the village smith, in some parts, still made practically everything in metal the countryman wanted—including knives, forks, clocks and watches.

"A tuk t'chain un hook upalong to smith and told 'en to put a point on 'en," said a Dorset villager. "Smith, 'ee says hook be too bent to sharpen but I told 'en his father and his father afore 'en 'd put a point on this there hook, un 'ee 'd better do 'en t'same if 'ee wanted to keep custom. And 'ee did 'en tu."[2]

Branding irons for marking the farmers' implements and beasts were among the products of the rural smith, and at least two parish smithies in Jersey have on their doors the trial impressions of branding implements with which the growers

---

[1] *Crafts of the Countryside* (E. J. Stowe).
[2] *Bournemouth Daily Echo*, May 3rd, 1950.

once stamped their potato barrels. At one, at St. Martin's, the smith is Charles Robins.

Even in the twentieth century, the rural blacksmith in the remote areas has still been making kitchen equipment and household utilities spasmodically, though not to the extent of the eighteenth century, when cranes, shovels, tongs and much else were the work of the local smith. Ella Pontefract and Marie Hartley could still find a local blacksmith who could make a new gate for the garden or a grate for the fire; he came of a long line of blacksmiths; his great-grandfathers and grandfather were smiths in Swaledale.[1] The champion farrier at the Royal

"While appreciating that the village blacksmith has often saved the day, I can't allow you to bat without the sanction of the selectors"—by NEB (By permission of Associated Newspapers Ltd.)

Show at Cambridge in 1951, a Scottish-born blacksmith from Wrexham, North Wales, represented a fourth generation of smithing, and began work at fourteen years of age in his father's forge at a shilling a week.

No doubt the smith's versatility and adaptability, plus his contact with the travelling public in earlier days, had much to do with the fact that he was usually a person of some weight in the village counsels—as well as in the cricket team. The Master Smith of Lyme Regis had his portrait painted by Whistler.

In an early nineteenth-century tract, quoted in *Hone's Everyday Book*, on "The arraigning and indicting of Sir John Barleycorn Kt.—printed by Timothy Tosspott", Vulcan, the blacksmith, called as a witness, deposed that Sir John had been a great enemy to him and his friends. "Many a time when I have been busy at my work, not thinking any harm to any man, having a firespark in my throat, I, going over to the sign of the Cup and Can for one pennyworth of ale," found Sir John, who broke his head, his face and almost all his bones, so that he was unable to work for three or four days,

[1] *Yorkshire Cottage.*

was left without a penny to support his family, and was scolded by his wife. But this is a gross libel on a generally respected craftsman—even though in 1825, a journeyman blacksmith of Horsham sold his wife for £2 5s., the purchaser taking one of the three children.

In point of fact, the smithy was often a rival to the village inn as a club. Through all the ages and in all countries, the village well has been the women's gossiping place.[1] That of the men has been either the bridge[2] or the forge, as persistently as the well with the women. The forge was the news rendezvous in the villages of ancient Greece; Barke, in *The Wind that Shakes the Barley*, pictures Robert Burns in discussions with his friends around the smithy fire; Ella Pontefract and Marie Hartley, in the present century, found the smithy in their Yorkshire village still the place for masculine gossip,[3] and Longfellow's picture of the children watching the sparks fly was perhaps even more true of the old country than the new. One can imagine the gusto with which a gloating group would watch a seventeenth-century smith make a scold's bridle![4]

Where the rural smith still functions, tradition yet holds sway. Anvil, hammer and forge have changed little through the centuries. The bellows may be replaced by an electric blower, but often it is still the old hand bellows, the lever made of ash. Frequently the handle of the bellows lever in English and Welsh smithies is a cow horn; the author has sought some traditional origin for this, but has only been told that it is convenient and prevents splinters from getting into the hand of the operator. Its use, however, is so general as to be intriguing. More often than not, the anvil rests on a rough block of wood, perhaps a section of a large tree-trunk, to which it is cramped.[5] The row of tools on the wall might well have been seen in the workshop of a Roman smith. The only gadget the blacksmith uses to test a bar for straightness is his keen experienced eye.[6] A few country smiths remember the wearing of a fringe to the apron,

[1] *See* the author's *Story of Water Supply.*
[2] *See* the author's *Story of the Bridge.*
[3] *Yorkshire Cottage.*
[4] But, judging from the forge stool preserved at Bridgwater Museum, customers at Weston Leyland had nothing else to do, while waiting, but to drive nails in it.
[5] The author has seen something similar in the Tyrol.
[6] The same applies to men who straighten steel tubes.

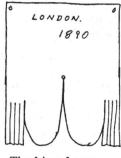

The fringed apron—
London, 1890

which another version of the old story alleges was awarded to the "King of Craftsmen" as a distinguishing sign by King Solomon himself;[1] fewer still wear one.

At one time, the blacksmith was horse doctor too. Some of the older smiths still possess a "balling iron", an iron frame containing a circle and an ellipse, which was applied to the horse's mouth; the animal's tongue being then drawn through the ellipse, the smith would thrust his arm through the circle into the horse's mouth and drop a "ball" of medicine behind the tongue. An alternative described to the author in a Dorset village, and used within living memory, was a sort of "popgun" which shot the pill into the horse's throat. Smiths also made and used an instrument for scraping a horse's throat. A growth of sagging flesh behind the teeth which prevented a young horse from eating was cured by the drastic application of a hot iron; the author has been assured that, so far from the horse rearing or kicking, at the first touch of the hot iron it became as though dazed. This sort of thing is now illegal and other methods have to be used.

Another blacksmith's job was "ringing" pigs; one old Buckinghamshire smith remembers ringing fifty-six in one day, at a charge of sevenpence per pig.[2]

If the shoeing smith has ceased to play the part of veterinary surgeon, he must still have a knowledge of horses and their "make-up". To get the certificate of the Worshipful Company of Farriers[3]—founded in 1356, incorporated by Royal Charter in 1674—which entitles him to call himself a "Registered Shoeing Smith", he must not only pass a shoeing test, but must have a knowledge of the anatomy of a horse's foot and leg.[4]

---

[1] Each kind of smith had a different pattern, and there also seem to have been "local fashions".

[2] Per Mr. F. T. Hand.

[3] In 1758, an act of common council imposed on all operative farriers the obligation of taking up the freedom of the company, but this rule has been abandoned in favour of a policy of encouragement and education.

[4] Poole Museum has an exhibit of shoes specially made for lame horses.

A young apprentice of a Dorset registered smith was able, too, to give an accurate history of the development of the horse's foot from prehistoric times, and of the horseshoe from the time when a strand of hemp was first wound around the horse's foot.

More than this, the expert shoeing smith must know the ways of horses. E. J. Stowe, in *Crafts of the Countryside*, quotes a case of a blacksmith who, when it was pointed out to him that the shoeing shed next his smithy was a mass of spiders and cobwebs, explained that he deliberately left them there to keep the flies down, since flies made horses' restive. A troublesome horse was often shod in a sort of cage of wood and chains, usually known as "stocks". One at the smithy at Upton Cross, in Dorset, was specially constructed for a vicious horse belonging to the Lees of Lytchett Matravers, and was only removed a few years back. They were used elsewhere in England, though none seem now to be extant. Stocks for oxen, with a boarded and thatched roof, on the island of Herm, in the Channel Islands, have outlived their usefulness, but remain as one of the sights of the island. During their occupation of Jersey, the German authorities suggested the erection of horse stocks to a smith of the island, and though not on their original site, they still remain, but the smith explains that he does not care about their use, since a restive horse is liable to slip on the cobbled paving in its struggles. The stocks were in common use in Germany, Belgium and France, where the smith, instead of holding the horse's hoofs himself, may have an assistant to do it for him or it is brought up and held by a roller at the end of the stocks.[1] Stocks were also, at one time, used in the British Army for shoeing those animals of notoriously uncertain behaviour, mules.

Today, the only fixtures of an English shoeing shed may be the rings or a bar to which the horses are tied.

Mr. Elmes, of Wareham, Dorset, was a smith who remembered and carried on old traditions and eschewed the modern trend towards oxy-acetylene and electric welding. His smithy bears outside the signs of his craft—the inevitable horseshoe and a wrought-iron flower. The shoeing shed is a cobbled chamber

[1] French smiths sometimes tie the horse's hoof to a post.

adjoining the forge, with a wooden manger at one end; the
horse's hoof rests on a tripod stand when it is not on the smith's
leather-aproned knee, and a box of nails and tools completes
the picture here. Through a door, one enters the forge itself.
One fire is "alive", with a twisting brick chimney leading upwards through the roof. Another is "dead". Both are provided
with hand bellows—each of these with the cow-horn handle.

At the back of the smithy hangs "G.R." in painted iron, and
an old print of a jovial bearded smith holding a child on his
shoulder beneath the smith's bunch of mistletoe. A modern
drilling machine at one end strikes a later note than the rest
of the tools—hammers of various kinds and sizes, tongs,
pincers, vices, the grindstone and a spare anvil. Over shoeing
shed and forge is a half-loft, carrying the stocks of rods and
bars for the smithy. Evidences of the diverse nature of the
smith's work lie or hang about—bicycle chains, horse and
pony shoes, picks, kettles, garden tools, but these are not all;
Mr. Elmes, for one thing, made the lamps of East Lulworth
church, the sort of job which was once a commonplace among
village smiths.

In parts of Wales, too, it is not so long since the smith
was making most of the domestic fittings for the Welsh country
house—kettle tilters, pot-hooks, cranes, hearth-irons, cauld-
rons, hooks, goffering irons, trivets, spits, rushlight holders, as
well as harrow tines, ploughshares, coulters, peat-cutters, har-
ness irons, wheel strokes, waggon-irons, and, says Dr. Peate,
in the National Museum of Wales' Guide to the Collection
illustrating Welsh Folk Crafts and Industries, "it is in these
ordinary domestic objects that the general excellency of rural
craftsmanship can be seen".

There is still a demand on smiths for wrought-iron gates,
some of them fine specimens of craftsmanship; the older smiths
claim that fire-welded gates have five or six times the life of
the welded product. Lamp standards, candlesticks and sconces
still come sometimes from the smithy; the author has a four-
socket wrought-iron candlestick made at North Stoneham
Smithy, Hampshire.[1] Wessex has smiths who can turn out fine
work. When the Forestry Commission instituted a competition
for the best billhook and slashhook, smiths entered from all

---

[1] The first circular saw is said to have been made there.

over the country and the hooks were exhibited at the Royal
Show at Shrewsbury; the first three prizes went to Hampshire
smiths.

Many a village smithy, today, works intermittently. Sometimes the smiths visit the farms with a travelling forge, to
shoe what horses there are at work.[1] A Dorsetshire smith relates how, at the end of the nineteenth century as an apprentice, he would walk two miles to a farm, put on a pair of horseshoes,[2] and get back before the forge opened, for sixpence a
time, but at one time large farms or groups of farms would
employ their own smiths. In Scandinavia, the forge is an
adjunct of the farm.

Shoes for riding horses are chamfered or grooved to prevent
them from being pulled off by suction in heavy ground. Usually,
nowadays, grooved iron or mild steel—wrought iron being
almost unobtainable—is bought for the purpose, but occasionally the smith still does the grooving by hand. Horses imported from Ireland often have their hind shoes removed for
the voyage, so that they do not injure one another; they then
have to be reshod on arrival in England. Many horses in Ireland, however, have their hind feet left unshod. Hind shoes
are more pointed than those for the fore feet.

Ox shoes, which, unlike horseshoes, are made in halves,
to suit the cloven hoof, have been rarely made in recent years
in this country.[3] Mr. Tucker, of Dorchester, is one who has
made them. Shoeing racehorses is a special job, aluminium[4] or
thin steel shoes being used. In America this job is in the hands
of a small ageing group of specialists. The *Saturday Evening
Post* (Philadelphia) for March 1, 1947, in a feature headed "The
Smith, a Scarce Man is He", stated that there were then, in
the United States, less than a hundred and seventy-five of
them, members of the Incorporated Association of Journeymen Horseshoers, and aged from sixty to eighty. Nobody but
these elderly smiths can shoe a racehorse, and they travel from
track to track, with a portable forge and anvils in their cars.

[1] Cairo farriers shoe horses in the street.
[2] A complete set of four shoes takes, I am told, an hour and a half to two
hours to make and fit.—F. W. R.
[3] Oxen, and even Devon cattle, were, however, ploughing on the Wiltshire
Downs within living memory and fairly recently in Sussex and at Cirencester.
[4] Stamped cold.

Trained in a three-year apprenticeship, completed by a final test similar to that in the guild system, they are well paid but often risk injury through the uncertain temper of racehorses. Expert and knowledgeable to the point of performing near-miracles, they are regarded as a "combination of seer and medicine man". So once again the New World echoes the traditions of the past.

Repair work to farm appliances is now often carried out by means of portable oxy-acetylene welding plants, though the older smiths, most of whom served five years or so as apprentices,[1] still prefer the forge-weld. Not long since, however, it was announced in the press that a five-ton mobile workshop, with oxy-acetylene and electric welding equipment, was to start a three weeks' tour to teach a hundred and eighty Cornish village blacksmiths modern methods—and Cornwall is the repository of many things long lost in the rest of England.

As Norman Wymer writes:

"No other craftsman has to make such instantaneous decisions or take such sudden and violent action on his materials. A woodworker can put everything down and begin again where he left off, but with the smith it is often a case of now or never. This factor, together with his complete mastery of horses during shoeing, probably accounts for the direct downright independence which is so familiar a feature of this craftsman. Perhaps it is the traditional spirit, too, and the atmosphere of his workshop—not infrequently an atmosphere in which history lingers—that prompts such workmanship and such versatility. Many of our present-day blacksmiths are carrying on a family job that has been handed down from generation to generation for hundreds of years, while their smithies are often hundreds of years old and must have many an interesting story to tell if only their walls could speak."

To which one would add, harking back to the Middle Ages, that the village smiths have a long record of freedom behind

---

[1] Because of a mistake in his apprenticeship indentures, Mr. Edward Hill, a Ripley, Derbyshire, blacksmith, who started his "three-year" apprenticeship in 1899, finds he will be an apprentice until 2002.

them to account for their independent spirit. It was the smith and his kind who won England back for the English from the Norman invaders, quietly but surely, in the Middle Ages. Pray God we may never lose it again, by force or by guile! And we still say "hammer and tongs" to indicate unflagging energy; hammer and sickle only come together when one or the other is not at its proper work.

The smithies, other than those which are mere appendages to some works, are getting fewer and fewer. To quote Dr. Iorwerth Peate on Wales, again:

> "today, carpenters, smiths, tailors and shoemakers have almost disappeared from the countryside. They ceased to be an integral element in the rural community. . . . It is exceptional today to find a craftsman who makes a complete plough."

Many, however, remain, sometimes in unexpected places. There were still three thousand smithies working in Britain in 1950, mostly one-man businesses, but many have been turned into petrol stations or repair depots for agricultural machinery. Usually when an old smith dies, his forge is abandoned or converted. A forge whose anvil rang in the ears of the author on his way to school, in a military town of no antiquity and with no rural associations, still works, though the farrier-sergeants of the old horsed regiments may no longer be needed in the adjoining camp.[1] There are smithies around the New Forest and in Dorset which do not need the sale of postcards, tourists' curiosity, or the making of miniature horseshoes "for luck", to keep them going. For the rest, we can but quote the Lincolnshire epitaph to one Thomas Tye, a blacksmith:

> My fire's extinct, my forge decayed,
> And in the dust my vice is laid,
> My coal is spent, my iron's gone,
> My nails are drawn, my work is done,
> My fyre-dryed corpse lies here at rest,
> My soul, like smoke, is soaring to the blest.

---

[1] Messrs. Sex and Sons, Send, Woking, though, made 30,000 horse shoes during the late war.

A COLOPHON

Sweet it is to write the end of any book.
As many, therefore, as shall read this book, pardon me,
I beseech you, if aught I have erred in accent acute
and grave, in apostrophe, in breathing or aspirate, and
may God save you all! Amen.

(Mediaeval.)

INDEX

A

Abingdon, 67
Africa, 18–25, 27, 28, 30–1, 33–6, 78, 89
Agni, 39, 41, 127, 131
Alcester, 67
Alfred, King, 76
America, 31, 78, 88, 142, 143–5, 153–4
Anvil, the, 15–16, 22, 27, 32, 41, 43–4, 51, 57, 62, 71, 77–8, 81, 85, 99, 101, 106, 110, 115, 117, 123–4, 126–30, 132, 135, 137, 145, 149, 152–3
Apprentices, 20, 65, 78, 84, 92, 115–16, 133–4, 154
Apron, the, 77, 85, 149–50
Arabs, 28, 32, 35, 36, 78, 120, 140
Aristotle, 40
Armada, the, 77–8
Armourers, 41, 45, 48–9, 51, 55–6, 58, 64, 87–92, 94–5, 100, 111, 128, 135
Arthur, King, and Arthurian legends, 57–8
Asia Minor, 14, 18, 26, 30, 38, 42
Athene, 41–2
Attila, 53
Austrian Tirol, 98, 149
Axes, 16–17, 20–1, 30, 35, 83

B

Babylon, 37, 84
Bakewell, Robert, 136
Balling iron, 150
Bards, 61–3, 127–9, 146
Basuto, 27
Bath, 89
Beaumaris Castle, 83
Belgium, 100, 111–12, 126, 135, 151
Bellows, 14, 20–4, 27, 30, 41, 44, 71, 81, 99, 109, 117, 124, 126–8, 149
Bells, 30, 44, 67, 90, 127, 133, 147
Beowulf, 48, 55–7
Berwick-on-Tweed, 105
Bible, The, 16, 17, 18, 32, 37, 106
Billhooks, 83, 86, 152
Birmingham, 88
Blacksmiths' Companies, 89–98, 105, 133, 137
Bladesmiths, 90, 95
Bodmin, 87
Bog-ore, 19

Borrow, George, 6, 39, 43, 46, 48, 117–18, 122–3, 127, 131, 144
Bournemouth, 145
Brands, 147
Brigit, 41, 62, 127
Bristol, 92, 136
British Museum, 44, 48, 70
Brittany, 73
Bronze, 13–16, 30, 51, 64, 121
Buckinghamshire, 105, 150
Bulgaria, 123
Burma, 22, 24, 27, 37–8
Burns, Robert, 60, 149

C

Candlesticks, 82, 103–4, 135, 152
Canterbury, 92–3
Carnarvon Castle, 82
Caste, 32–7
Cauldron, 17, 28, 86, 152
Caxton, 88
Celts, 17, 60–5, 67, 127, 129
Ceylon, 28
Charcoal, 14, 19, 20–1, 24, 52, 100, 122–5, 139–42
Charlemagne, 48, 58, 80
Chester, 89, 90, 92, 94–5, 133
Chesterfield, 90
China, 16, 17, 18, 139–40
Chisel, the, 16, 23, 44, 75–6, 81, 102, 117
Christ, 50, 95–6, 112–14, 118–21
Cid, The, 58–9
Cilicia, 18
Circassia, 39
Cirencester, 153
Cistercians, the, 67, 81
Clans, 24, 27, 64
Clement, St., 69, 74–9
Clocks, 87, 103–5, 135, 147
Coal, 93–4, 142, 155
Colchester, 85
Copper, 13, 14, 21, 42, 90, 118, 123–4, 133
Cornwall, 78, 87, 92, 130, 141, 154
Corsica, 140
Coventry, 92–8
Cow-horn, 149
Crete, 41–2
Cuchulain, 61–2
Culann, 62–3
Cumberland, 13, 102

157

Cutlers, 89–95, 142
Cycles, 146, 152
Cyclops, 39, 43–4
Cyprus, 44

D

Danaans, the, 61
Davies family, 136
Demons, 27, 28, 115–16 (*see* also Devil)
Denmark, 38, 55–7, 128
Dentistry, 29, 91
Devil, the, 28–9, 50, 68–72, 98, 106–16
Dietrich, 55
Door fittings, 44, 80–2, 102
Dorset, 28, 73, 77, 85, 103, 105, 130, 145–8, 150–1, 153, 155
Dunstan, St., 50, 66–71, 92, 127
Dwarfs, 46–9, 53, 58

E

Edgar, King, 67
Edney, William, 136
Egwin, St., 66
Egypt, 14, 23, 26, 51, 140, 153
Eloi, St. (St. Leger, St. Eloysius, St. Loy), 69–73, 91–2, 113
England, 44, 48–9, 54, 66–72, 74–9, 80–105, 118–19, 124–5, 130, 135–8, 139–42, 144–56
Epitaphs, 102, 155
Esthonia, 83
Ethelwald, Bishop, 67
Etna, Mount, 43, 78
Eton College, 83
Excalibur (*see* Swords)

F

Fairies, 28, 63
Fans, 23
Farriers, 49, 72, 83, 86, 90–2, 102–3, 106, etc., 117, 144–5, 150–1
Farriers' Company, 79, 86, 93, 150
Files, 23, 102, 118, 133
Finland, 41, 130
Flanders (*see* Belgium)
Forest of Dean, 80, 101
Forges, 18, 20–2, 25, 27, 42, 43, 46–8, 61, 63–4, 67, 71, 73, 75, 78–9, 81, 86, 100–1, 106–16, 117, 119–24, 126–8, 132, 137, 139, 141–2, 155
Formorians, the, 61
Formosa, 18, 22
Founders, 89–91
Fountains Abbey, 81
France, 49, 54, 58, 71, 73, 90, 121–3, 130, 140, 151

Frey, 46, 53
Furness Abbey, 81

G

Gates, 100, 135–6, 147–8, 152
Geoffrey of Monmouth, 49, 58
George, St., 113
Germany, 47, 53–4, 82, 87, 98, 101–2, 122, 133–5
Giants, 50, 55–6
Girdlers, 90–1, 93–4
Gloucester, 90
Gobha, Goban, Goibhnean, Goibnu, 60–64
Gods, 18, 27, 29, 39–45, 46–50, 107
Goldsmiths, 15, 25, 39, 41–3, 46–7, 49, 61, 64, 66–7, 69, 71, 73, 75, 89–91, 95, 100, 121, 127
Gow, 64, 87–8, 128
Greece, 16–17, 23, 31, 39–44, 121–3, 131
Gretna Green, 100, 131–2
Guilds, 30, 33, 69, 83, 86, 89–98, 133–4
Gypsies, 16, 30, 35–7, 103, 106–11, 113, 117–25, 128–30

H

Haddads, 35–7, 118
Hammers, 15–16, 21–3, 27, 30, 32, 41–4, 46, 48, 50, 61, 64, 76, 78, 80–1, 83, 85–6, 88, 99–101, 106, 109–11, 114–15, 117, 119, 122–3, 126, 130, 133, 135, 137, 143–5, 149, 152, 155
Hampshire, 44, 74–5, 77, 84, 92, 94, 100, 125, 130, 139, 141, 145, 152–3, 155
Hearth furniture, 86–7, 100–1, 103, 148, 152
Hephaestus, 40–5, 46
Hereford, 80, 92–3, 95, 142
Herm, 151
Hertfordshire, 44
Hesiod, 127
Heuss, George, 135
Hoes, 21, 25–31, 38
Holland, 101, 135
Horse shoes, 26, 79–83, 90, 92, 102–3, 117, 128, 145–6, 150–1, 153, 155
Hungary, 121–4, 130
Hunzas, the, 22, 25, 37, 129

I

Iliad, the, 39
Ilmarinen, 41
India, 14, 23, 25, 27, 29, 32, 37, 51, 127–9, 131

Ingelri, 54
Irak, 37, 84, 118, 129
Ireland, 14–15, 29, 60–64, 153
Iron and ironworking, 15–20, 27, 40–5, 46–9, 51–4, 63–4, 66, 67, 80–6, 93, 100–2, 133–7, 152
Ironmongers, 85, 89–91, 124
Israel, 16–18, 30, 32, 37, 121
Italy, 28, 43, 78, 91, 122, 124, 140
Itinerant smiths, 15–16, 43, 60, 81, 121, 133–4, 153

J

Jael, 18
Japan, 27
Jarlshof, 15–16
Java, 31
Jersey, 147, 151
Jews, the, 16–18, 30, 32, 37, 58, 119
Jugo-Slavia, 123–4, 129

K

Kenites, the, 18
Kent, 68, 74, 100, 101, 141
Kenya, 19, 22–3, 30, 33, 34, 36
Korea, 31, 146

L

Lakhers, the, 24–5, 31
Lalouale, 36
Lambas, the, 20, 22–3, 33, 129
Lameness, 40, 47, 122
Lapps, the, 28
Layamon, 58
Legends, 35, 40–5, 46–65, 67–9, 72–7, 106–16, 118–21
Leicestershire, 145
Leighton, Thomas of, 81
Lemnos, 40, 43
Lincoln and Lincolnshire, 90, 145, 155
Lipari islands, 43
Locksmiths, 88, 92, 100, 123, 133
Loki, 46, 49
London, 69, 78, 81, 85–7, 91–4, 135
Longfellow, 19, 26, 126, 130, 143–5, 149
Loriners, 88, 90–1, 96
Lucretius, 13
Ludlow, 90
Lugh, 61, 127

M

Macedonia, 122–3
Magic, 26–31, 49, 51–9, 60–1, 66, 122, 128
Mahomet, 35
Mallory, 57
Martin, St., 79

Mashonas, the, 34
Masons, 75–6, 82–3, 88, 123–4, 136
Matsys, Quentin, 135
Mesopotamia (see Irak)
Meteoric iron, 14, 26
Michael, St., 53
Monasteries, 67, 73, 81–2
Morocco, 28
Moxon, Joseph, 101–2
Musicians and musical instruments, 49, 61–2, 69, 118, 121, 126–30
Mystery Plays, 94–8
Myths (see Legends)

N

Nagas, the, 22, 24, 37
Nails, 18, 28, 33, 80–1, 84, 86, 88, 90, 92, 95, 97, 103, 114, 118–21, 152, 155
Neolithic period, 14
Newcastle-on-Tyne, 92, 142
New Forest, 100, 125, 130, 141, 155
Northamptonshire, 80
Norwich, 90, 95
Nuremburg, 135

O

Oakham, 84
Oberammergau, 98
Odin, 46, 48–9, 53, 54
Odyssey, 39, 43
Og, King of Bashan, 17
Oliver, 58
Olympus, 40–3
Oxford and Oxfordshire, 68, 85, 104
Ox shoes, 83, 153

P

Palestine, 16, 30, 37, 118–21
Patrick, St., 29
Payment, 20–1, 24, 25, 43, 49, 83–5, 92, 96–7, 103–5, 140, 153
Persia, 140
Peter, St., 50, 113–14
Philistines, 37
Phrygia, 14, 30
Plough, 17, 31, 38, 44, 59, 80, 84, 85, 88, 106, 127, 155
Poland, 31
Poole, 85, 103, 146
Preston, 90
Priests, 27, 30–1, 67, 84, 132
Prometheus, 42
Pythagoras, 126–8

R

Regin, 49, 54, 127
Rings, 29, 46–8, 63, 123, 131
Roland, 58

Rome and Romans, 13, 30, 40, 45, 53, 89, 118–24, 139
Rumania, 122–4, 129
Runes, 49, 52–4, 58–9, 128
Rural Industries Bureau, 137
Russia, 37, 54, 115–16, 130

S

Sandgate, 83
Scandinavia, 19, 46–57, 80, 82, 101, 113–15, 124, 131, 153
Scotland, 15–16, 28, 57, 62–3, 64–5 66–7, 78, 87–8, 92, 122, 125, 131–3, 146, 148–9
Scott, Sir Walter, 64, 87–8
Shans, the, 38
Sheffield, 14, 17
Shrewsbury, 90, 153
Signs, 113, 133, 138, 147, 151
Sigurd, Siegfried, 49, 54–5, 127–8
Silchester, 44
Silver, 25, 42, 47, 67–71
Sinclairs, 64
Smelting, 13–18, 19–23, 81, 100, 141–2
Smetse Smee, 111–14, 126
Solomon, King, 30, 74–6
Somerset, 73, 85, 89, 149
Sorcery, 29, 54, 60, 122, 124, 132
Spain, 19, 58–9, 101–2, 122–3, 130, 139–40
Spears, 17, 18, 53, 61
Spurriers, 86, 89–91, 94, 96, 133
Steel, 28, 47, 60, 78, 80, 83, 101–2, 123, 149
Stigand, Bishop, 67
Stocks, 151
Stromboli, 43
Superstitions, 26–31, 35
Sussex, 68, 74, 77, 81, 83, 100–1, 141–2, 147, 149, 153
Sutton Hoo, 49–50
Switzerland, 29
Swords, 16–17, 31, 36, 43–4, 47–9, 51–9, 60–1, 63, 88, 118, 128

T

Taunton, 85
Thor., 46–50, 131
Tijou, Jean, 135
Tin, 14, 122, 124–5

Tompion, 105
Tongs, 23, 41–4, 48, 50, 61, 68, 72, 78, 101–2, 106, 122–3, 152, 155
Tuaregs, the, 32, 129
Tubal-Cain, 16, 18, 60, 76, 80
Turkey, 123, 140
Twyford, Hants, 74–5, 77–8
Tyr, 52
Tyre, 18

U

Ulfbert, 54

V

Veterinary Surgery, 79, 103, 150
Vices, 81, 101–2, 155
Volsungs, 54
Volund (see Wayland)
Vulcan, 39, 45–6, 62, 78–9, 85, 99, 121, 129, 148

W

Wachagga, the, 22, 24, 33
Wales, 31, 63, 82–3, 106, 136, 142, 146, 148–9, 152
Wareham, 77, 151–2
Watch, the, 90, 94
Wayland, 46–9, 55, 58, 60
Weald, the, 81, 100, 141
Wheels, 44, 67, 92, 97, 144
Wigan, 105
Williams, John, 146
Wiltshire, 147, 153
Wincanton, 73
Winchester, 92, 94
Wiredrawers, 90, 93, 133
Witchcraft, 28, 57, 122
Women, 20, 29, 83–4
Wood fuel, 19, 23, 31, 139–42
Woolwich, 78

X

Xenophon, 40

Y

York and Yorkshire, 14, 17, 81, 83, 92, 95, 101, 147–9

Z

Zeus, 40, 42, 78

CPSIA information can be obtained
at www.ICGtesting.com
Printed in the USA
BVHW040313281022
650361BV00008B/586

9 781446 508558